Because I Never Give up

Simran K. Saini

Published by: Simran K. Saini

Edition 1

To My Younger Self & Karan and Jack

Contents

About the Author

Simran is a London-based accountant, author, philosopher, social activist and meditation guide who turned personal pain into purpose. Born from a childhood of silence and struggle, she now teaches others how to find strength in their scars and rise as the heroes of their lives. Her voice is soft with compassion, yet fierce with truth, guiding readers toward healing, power, and self-mastery.

Purpose of the Book

This book is a heartfelt exploration of my own life's most challenging moments; moments where I felt like giving up, when life's setbacks felt too overwhelming to overcome. Through the stories of my childhood and the formative years up to age 21, I aim to share not just the pain, but also the profound lessons I've learned from those struggles. This book is a reminder that every challenge, every setback, and even the harshest people in our lives serve as stepping stones toward becoming our best selves.

I want to show readers that failure doesn't define us, but it shapes us into who we are meant to be. My purpose in writing this book is to encourage anyone who feels trapped in a dark moment; those who believe they're too broken, too lost, or too far gone to change; to recognize that the very things that hurt them can be the forces that help them grow. I want my readers to discover their inner strength, build their resilience, and find the power to turn every obstacle into an opportunity.

Through this book, I aim to provide a practical, action-oriented guide to help readers navigate through their own struggles, just as I've learned to do. This isn't just a motivational read, but a blueprint to take tangible action and embrace personal transformation. At the end of each lesson, I will share concrete, step-by-step methods that readers can apply to their own lives, ensuring they don't just read about change but actively create it.

By the end of this book, my goal is for readers to feel empowered, equipped, and full of emotional strength and toughness. I want them to see every challenge as a chance to grow, to welcome adversity with a positive attitude, and to walk forward with confidence in their ability to shape their future.

This book is my gift to my younger self, the one who struggled, doubted, and felt lost, but who ultimately found a way out. I want anyone who feels they are in a similar situation to know that there is a path forward; one filled with hope, possibility, and the courage to embrace every challenge with open arms.

Section: 1

Breaking the Chains

I have a great memory, and I remember nearly every moment of my childhood, even from when I was as young as four or five. But there's one moment, one event that stands out more than any other. Everyone has a moment when their world feels like it's falling apart. Mine came when I was just 6 years old.

I grew up in a big joint family. Our house was always filled with people; my grandparents, my parents, and my two uncles, who were my father's younger brothers. It was a lively home, full of conversations, laughter, and the sounds of daily life. At just five years old, I was the only child in the house, but I never felt alone. My uncles were playful and full of energy, always joking around. I loved watching them, fascinated by their carefree nature.

Back then, my father was my hero. He was a hardworking man, strict but caring. Whenever he held my hand, I felt safe. My mother was a kind and gentle woman. She would softly run her fingers through my hair as I fell asleep. Her warmth made me feel loved and protected. Though we didn't have a lot of money, our home was rich with love and togetherness.

But as I grew older, I began to notice a change in my mother. The warmth in her eyes slowly faded. She seemed tired, both physically and emotionally. I was too young to understand it then, but now I know why. My grandparents, especially my grandmother, were harsh with her. In traditional Indian households, it's common for daughters-in-law to carry the heavy load of housework. My mother was no exception. She cooked, cleaned, and cared for everyone without a break. She had no support, no one to lean on. Day after day, the endless labour and mistreatment wore her down.

I saw her kindness turn into bitterness. Her soft voice became sharp. She no longer had the patience for my childhood mischief. I didn't understand that her heart was breaking under the weight of constant exhaustion and neglect. All I knew was that she was changing-and so was my relationship with her.

Still, my father's presence remained my comfort. I wanted to be close to him, to make him proud. But everything changed the day we visited the astrologer.

One morning, my parents took me by the hand and told me we were going to see an astrologer. I was just six years old, too young to understand what it meant. I was excited to go out with him. Holding my father's hand, I walked along the dusty road, looking up at him with admiration. He was my whole world back then.

We arrived at a small, dimly lit room. The astrologer sat on a wooden chair, dressed in a simple white kurta pajama. His face is a blur in my memory. I was too young to recall his features but I distinctly remember his attire. It was the traditional outfit worn by many men in

India and for some reason, it made him appear more authoritative, almost priest-like.

When we arrived, I spotted the landline phone sitting on a small table near the astrologer's desk. In the late 90's, landlines were common in homes, and I was fascinated by them. I loved pressing the buttons, pretending to have long conversations with imaginary friends. I would do this at home all the time, babbling into the receiver with wild stories, laughing at my own make-believe jokes. So, naturally, I couldn't resist doing the same at the astrologer's house.

While my father and the astrologer spoke in low tones, I crept over to the phone, my tiny fingers quickly dialling random numbers, giggling softly. I was lost in my little game, chatting away with my fictitious friends, when suddenly, my father's sharp voice cut through the room.

"Stop it! Don't touch other people's things. It's bad manners!" he scolded, his eyes narrowing with disapproval.

My hands froze mid-air. Embarrassed, I slowly placed the receiver back. I didn't understand why he was so stern-it was just a phone-but I lowered my head and shuffled back to the wooden bench where I had been sitting. My legs swung back and forth restlessly, too short to reach the ground.

The astrologer, meanwhile, barely glanced at me. He was deeply engrossed in writing something on a small, worn-out booklet. His brows were furrowed in concentration as he analyzed what I now realize must have been my father's birth chart. Back then, I had no idea what he was doing-it just seemed like a lot of squiggles and symbols. I stared at him, curious but clueless.

After a while, he finally lifted his head. His eyes shifted towards me, and then, with a calm yet deliberate tone, he spoke the words that would change the course of my childhood.

"Listen carefully," he addressed my father, his voice steady and certain, "never trust this girl."

My small ears perked up at the mention of me. For a brief moment, I felt a strange excitement. I thought he was going to say something nice, maybe even call me special. But his next words crushed that innocent hope.

"She may be your daughter, but when you grow old, she will not stand by you. She will betray you."

Betray. A word far too heavy for a child's heart. I didn't know exactly what it meant, but I could feel the weight in his voice. His eyes were cold, unwavering, as if he were reading from a divine script, declaring a fate that couldn't be altered.

I turned to my father, searching for reassurance, but instead, I saw his face darken. His jaw tightened, and his eyes narrowed with suspicion, as if the man's words had unlocked a hidden doubt in him. He didn't say anything to me at that moment, but the shift was unmistakable. I could feel it.

From that day onward, I became a suspect in my father's eyes. The innocence of being his child was tainted by the astrologer's prophecy. Every time I made a mistake-whether I accidentally spilled water on the floor, forgot to complete a chore, or answered back with a hint of defiance-my father would bring it up.

"You'll be a shame to me," he would say, shaking his head in disappointment. "One day, you'll turn your back on me, just like he predicted."

At first, I didn't understand why he was suddenly so cold. I tried harder to impress him-being extra obedient, eagerly helping my mother, and watching him carefully to avoid triggering his anger. But it never seemed to be enough. The seed of doubt had already been planted, and it grew with every passing day.

And so, at the age of six, I unknowingly became the villain in my father's eyes-a child with a destiny already written in betrayal. Yet, in my heart, I knew I was nothing like the girl the astrologer described. I loved my father with all my being.

As I grew older, the weight of that prophecy never left me. It lingered like a shadow, following me through every mistake, every word spoken in anger, and every glance that seemed filled with distrust. The prophecy-the one that foretold I would betray my father-became an unspoken rule in our home. My father, though loving in his own way, always seemed distant. He would push me harder, expecting perfection in everything I did, as if he believed that his fate was tied to my actions.

The pressure built. I wanted so desperately to prove that I wasn't the person the astrologer had predicted. I became more obedient, tried to be the ideal child-careful not to anger him, careful not to do anything that would confirm his fears. But the more I tried to live up to the prophecy's opposite, the more I felt trapped in its grasp. It was like being tied to a string that someone else was pulling. No matter what I did, the more I felt like I was going to fall short of their expectations.

And then came the years of adolescence, when the clash between my independent thoughts and my father's beliefs became impossible to ignore. I started questioning things-everything. I was curious about the world beyond the walls of our home, and slowly, the blind faith that had been instilled in me began to crumble.

By the time I was a teenager, I could no longer swallow the superstitions that had shaped my childhood. I had begun to see them for what they were-stories made up to control, to confine, to keep people in line. My father's blind belief in astrology, the constant warnings of karma and divine punishment, had stifled my ability to think for myself. I wanted to break free.

One day, as I sat across from my father at the dinner table, the subject of astrology came up once again. My father, as usual, spoke about his latest astrological readings-how the stars aligned in his favour, how the upcoming planetary movements would bring good fortune. It wasn't anything new, but this time, something inside me snapped.

"Dad, why do you believe all this? Why do you let these things control your life? Can't you see it doesn't make sense?" I asked, my voice shaking but firm.

He stopped eating, his spoon hovering mid-air, and stared at me. His eyes, once filled with care, were now cold, distant. "You don't understand," he said sharply. "You will. But not until you realize the consequences of doubting these things."

I felt my heart race as I looked at him. The moment I had feared was finally here. I was challenging him, something I had never dared to do before. But in that moment, something inside me shifted. I wasn't afraid anymore. I wasn't the little girl who had to stay quiet and obey.

"You've always said that questioning these beliefs is bad," I said, my voice gaining strength. "But what if the real punishment is living your life based on fear, on things you don't even understand? Why can't we just live without worrying about what some stars or planets tells us? What about logic? What about the here and now?"

My father's face flushed with anger, his grip on the spoon tightening. "You'll regret this," he muttered. "You will bring misfortune upon yourself. And when it happens, don't come crying to me for help. You'll see the truth one day."

His words, filled with bitterness and fear, stung. But strangely, they didn't scare me anymore. They sounded hollow, empty. It was as if I had finally come to see through the veil of superstition that had clouded my world for so long.

The argument ended there, but the tension between us never truly left. From that moment, my father distanced himself from me even more. I became the rebel, the one who refused to accept the way things had always been. I was no longer the obedient daughter who followed the rules. I was the one who questioned everything.

But deep inside, I still loved him. No matter how much he pushed me away, I couldn't forget that he was the man who had raised me, who had provided for me. Despite his rigid beliefs and harsh words, he was still my father, and that bond couldn't easily be broken.

Over the years, I tried to find a balance. I still sought his approval, still longed for his love, but I also knew that I could no longer live under the weight of his expectations. I had to follow my own path, even if it meant going against everything he had taught me.

I could never change his mind. He would always hold onto his faith in astrology, and I would always question it. But I didn't need him to agree with me anymore. I had found my own strength, my own voice, and that was more than enough.

I forgave him-because holding onto anger wouldn't bring me peace. But I also knew that I couldn't live my life trying to please someone who would never understand me. I had to let go, not just of the superstitions, but also of the expectations that had tied me to the past.

I was free.

The Awakening

As I stepped into adulthood, I found myself torn between the child I once was, trying to meet the expectations of a father steeped in his superstitions, and the adult I was becoming-someone who needed to carve her own path, free from fear and imposed beliefs. The journey of self-discovery was both liberating and painful. I started to see the world not as a series of predestined events written in the stars but as a canvas of possibilities, where every choice mattered and where mistakes were simply part of the process. I didn't need astrology or divine predictions to shape my future. I was the architect of my own destiny.

But even as I tried to break free, there was always a part of me that missed the simplicity of my childhood, when things felt certain, when answers came easily. But adulthood didn't come with clear answers. It came with questions, with challenges, with the need to navigate a world that didn't always make sense. And in this search for meaning, I began to see that life was about balance-finding harmony between what we can control and what we can't, between our dreams and the reality we face.

Around this time, I became deeply interested in philosophy and logic, seeking knowledge in books and lectures that challenged the beliefs I had grown up with. I met people who were also trying to find their own way, some of them also breaking free from restrictive beliefs. I started asking myself, "What if everything I had been taught about fate, about life's direction, was wrong? What if we could be the creators of our own stories?" This curiosity led me to new perspectives, allowing me to see the world in shades of gray rather than black and white.

But I knew my father wouldn't understand this shift in me. The last time we spoke about it, his words echoed in my mind: "You'll regret this." And though I never wanted to prove him wrong for the sake of it, part of me realized that by living authentically, by questioning and challenging, I was building the life I wanted-one that was mine, not dictated by superstitions or the fear of punishment.

Over time, my father's harshness began to fade, not because he stopped believing in astrology, but because I stopped trying to change him. We learned to co-exist in our differences. I stopped seeking his approval in everything I did, stopped expecting him to understand my choices. This didn't mean I loved him any less, but I realized that true love doesn't require agreement-it requires acceptance.

I began to forgive myself for the years spent living in fear of his disappointment, and slowly, I let go of the guilt that had weighed heavily on my shoulders for so long. I could no longer carry the burden of trying to be someone I wasn't just to gain approval. The only person whose approval I needed was my own.

The Journey Ahead

And so, the years passed. The girl who had once feared the prophecy that her father believed in was no longer afraid. I embraced my independence, made my own decisions, and stood firm in the belief that life was a series of choices; choices that would shape who I was, not the stars or the planets. But even as I walked this path, the journey didn't come without its own set of challenges. Life was still full of twists and turns. Yet, I had learned to trust myself more than ever before. I learned that it was okay to not have all the answers, to not always know what the future held.

But I also knew one thing for certain: I would never stop questioning. I would never stop seeking the truth, no matter how uncomfortable it made others. My curiosity was my strength; my ability to think for myself was my power. And with this power, I felt free; free to live life on my own terms.

Looking back, I see how much that experience shaped my perception of life. At the time, I was consumed by fear, confusion, and doubt. But as I grew, I realized that this story wasn't just mine-it was a part of a much larger narrative that many of us experience. We all face moments of uncertainty and hardship, where it feels like the world is closing in around us. But what I learned, from that painful chapter, is that those challenges do not define us. They only prepare us for something greater.

It's during the darkest times that we have the most potential to grow. I now know that every obstacle we face has a purpose: to teach us the strength we never thought we had. If you're going through your own tough times right now, remember this: the greatest growth comes from the most difficult experiences. Your challenges are not here to stop you; they are here to prepare you for the greatness that lies ahead.

Lesson 1

Every Journey Comes with Struggles

"Every step forward carries its own weight and no journey is free of struggle, but every struggle shapes the strength to continue."

We all face struggles in life and some feel like insurmountable walls, while others leave scars deep in our hearts. For me, one of the hardest challenges was growing up under the shadow of a prediction made by an astrologer. Every time I failed or made a mistake, I could hear those words echo in my mind, making me feel worthless. I felt trapped, as if my past had a stranglehold on my future.

But here's the truth we often forget: Pain is not the enemy.

It's natural to want to avoid pain, to suppress it or bury it deep inside. But when we run from it, we miss the opportunity to learn and grow. Pain, when faced head-on, becomes a powerful tool for personal transformation. In fact, research shows that resilience; the ability to bounce back after hardship is one of the strongest predictors of success in life. Psychologist Carol Dweck, in her book *Mindset*, emphasizes that a "growth mindset" allows us to see challenges as opportunities for growth, not as roadblocks.

The struggles we experience in life do not define us unless we allow them to. Our past can only shape us if we let it.

The Power of Pain

When I was younger, I didn't understand this concept. It's hard to imagine that any good can come from pain when you're in the middle of it. But over time, I realized that my pain wasn't meant to break me; it was meant to build me. It was teaching me how to be resilient, how to persevere, and how to believe in myself, even when no one else did.

Viktor Frankl, a Holocaust survivor and psychiatrist, wrote in his book *Man's Search for Meaning* that even in the worst of circumstances, we have the power to choose how we respond to suffering. My pain reminded me that my real power was in how I chose to respond to it. I could let it define me, or I could rise above it.

Every time I faced rejection, heartbreak, or harsh criticism, especially from those I loved, I had a choice: I could let their opinions define me, or I could fight back. This wasn't easy. Moving forward felt like an uphill battle. But I kept going. I refused to let the judgments of others control my life. The more I hurt, the more determined I became. With each painful experience, I grew stronger.

Building Strength from Struggles

Looking back now, I can see that those painful experiences didn't destroy me, they shaped me. Every scar is proof of the strength I gained. Every rejection or misunderstanding was an opportunity for growth. The pain didn't break me; it made me tougher, wiser, and more determined. And here's the most important lesson I learned: my worth is not determined by others' opinions of me. My worth is mine to define.

This is the foundation of resilience: understanding that pain, while inevitable, does not control you. Your struggles are just parts of your story; they are not the whole story. The pain you've experienced does not define your future unless you let it.

You Are Not Your Pain

So, to you, the reader, let me say this: You are not your pain.

The struggles you face today are not the end of your journey. They are part of your story, but not the whole story. You have the power to decide how your struggles shape you. Healing and growing take time, but each time you rise above your pain, you become stronger. Every time you refuse to give up, you are proving to yourself that you are capable of so much more than you ever thought possible.

Practical Steps to Move through Pain

1. **Acknowledge Your Pain:** Take a few moments every day to reflect on your emotions and how you're handling your pain. This could be as simple as acknowledging that you're feeling overwhelmed or stressed, or as significant as recognizing a moment when you chose to persevere despite hardship. This simple acknowledgment helps you gain control over your emotions and keeps you from feeling overwhelmed.

Example:"I recognized I was feeling sad today, but I chose to take care of myself by going for a walk."

2. **Reframe Your Perspective on Pain:** Reframing is about changing the way you view pain. Instead of seeing it as something that's happening to you, ask yourself, "What can I learn from this experience?" or "How can this challenge help me grow?"

Example: If you experience a setback at work, you could reframe it from "I failed, and this is the end of my career" to "This is an opportunity to learn and improve." Shifting your perspective transforms challenges into growth opportunities.

3. **Use Pain to Build Resilience:** Start journaling about your struggles and the strengths you discover in yourself. Reflect on how you handled a recent challenge. What did you do

well? What did you learn about yourself? Journaling is a powerful tool to track your growth and reminds you of your resilience.

Example:"Today, I stayed calm during a heated discussion with a colleague. I kept my composure and respected my boundaries, even though I was triggered."

Remember, your journey is yours to shape. Every struggle, every hardship, and every painful moment holds the potential to make you stronger. Embrace your struggles as opportunities to grow. Stand tall and decide that your future belongs to you.

Lesson 2

Embrace the Power of Self-Belief: Let Go of External Validation

"When you believe in yourself, the need for others to believe in you fades. True power begins where external validation ends."

For years, I sought approval from someone whose opinion I valued above all others, my father. I believed that his approval would validate my worth, that his words of pride would be the key to feeling complete. I thought that if I could just meet his expectations, I would finally feel like I was enough. I was stuck in a constant cycle of striving for perfection, hoping that one day I would hear those words: "I'm proud of you."

But over time, I came to a powerful realization: no amount of external approval can ever fill the void left by self-doubt. I had been chasing something fleeting, validation from others, while completely ignoring the most important source of validation: my own.

The Trap of External Validation

For years, I handed over the keys to my self-worth, allowing others' opinions to shape who I was. Praise was temporary. Compliments were fleeting. I would feel good for a moment, only to be left hungry for more. And when criticism came, it cut deep, too deep. My identity was fragile, built on the unstable foundation of what others thought of me. This is a trap many of us fall into, one that psychologists have found leads to chronic insecurity and anxiety.

According to Kristin Neff, a leading researcher on self-compassion, seeking external validation often leads to emotional instability. When we rely on others to define our worth, we are at the mercy of their ever-changing opinions.

The Road to Self-Belief

But here's the truth I discovered: I didn't need anyone else to validate my worth. It was always mine to claim. No one, no matter how much I loved them, had the power to dictate who I was or how I felt about myself. The moment I stopped waiting for others to tell me I was good enough was the moment I began to truly believe in my own worth.

The journey to self-belief isn't easy. It's filled with doubts, fears, and the occasional setback. But with each small step I took toward trusting myself, I became stronger. I began showing up for myself every day, even when the world seemed to say otherwise. I learned that self-belief isn't just a thought; it's a practice.

Why Self-Belief Matters

Research shows that self-compassion and self-belief are closely linked to emotional resilience. According to Dr. Carol Dweck, a psychologist renowned for her work on mindset, those who cultivate a belief in their abilities,no matter the challenges they face,are more likely to succeed and grow. Self-belief isn't about blind confidence; it's about trusting your ability to overcome adversity, even when it feels impossible.

Breaking Free from the Validation Trap

When you rely on others to tell you that you're enough, you're constantly seeking something outside yourself. But when you stop seeking approval and start believing in yourself, you become unstoppable. You stop measuring your value by others' opinions and start living authentically, rooted in your own sense of worth.

Here's the key: The most powerful validation you can ever receive is the one you give yourself. And when you truly believe in your worth, the world will no longer hold the power to break you. It will only witness your rise.

Practical Steps to Build Self-Belief

1. **Identify Sources of Validation** Start by observing moments when you seek validation from others. For a week, track instances when you find yourself checking social media for likes, asking for reassurance, or waiting for compliments. This practice will help you identify patterns and triggers.

   Ask yourself:

- What prompted me to seek approval at this moment?

- How did I feel before and after seeking it?

2. **Reaffirm Your Worth** Write down a list of your strengths and positive traits. This could include qualities like "creativity," "resilience," or "kindness." Then, read this list out loud every morning. Reaffirm your worth daily.

   Example affirmations:

   "I am resilient and capable of overcoming challenges."
   "I am worthy of respect and love, just as I am."

By reaffirming your value regularly, you'll internalize these truths and start believing in your worth, regardless of external feedback.

3. **Create Boundaries with External Validation** Set aside time each day for activities that don't require anyone else's approval. This could be writing, drawing, exercising, or simply taking time for yourself. Do it purely for your own satisfaction.

   Ask yourself afterward:

- Did I feel the need to seek external approval? Why or why not?
- What did it feel like to do this just for me?

Your journey, your dreams, and your success are yours alone. No one can define them for you. Stop seeking validation from others. You don't need anyone's permission to believe in yourself. You are already enough. When you believe in yourself, you become unstoppable. And once you do, you'll realize that the only validation you ever truly need is the one you give yourself. The world will only witness your rise.

Lesson 3

Self-Awareness Leads to Empowerment

The moment you understand yourself is the moment you stop being powerless. Self-awareness is where true empowerment begins.

For years, I felt like a passenger in my own life, drifting along with the current of circumstances, unable to steer the ship. Whether it was the expectations of others, my past mistakes, or the situations life threw my way, I felt powerless to change anything. It wasn't until I realized one simple truth that everything changed: I had the power to choose how I responded to every situation.

Self-awareness isn't about criticizing yourself for past decisions or living in regret. It's about understanding your thoughts, emotions, and behaviours in the present moment, without judgment. It's the key that unlocks the door to your own power. The moment I started observing my reactions with curiosity, rather than judgment, I gained control over my life.

The Power of Self-Awareness

Self-awareness is the foundation of emotional intelligence, a concept popularized by Daniel Goleman in the mid-1990s. In his groundbreaking book *Emotional Intelligence,* Goleman explains how being in tune with your own emotions and understanding your triggers can fundamentally alter the way you experience life. The more aware we become of our thoughts and emotions, the more control we gain over our reactions. This shift from automatic responses to conscious choices is where empowerment begins.

When I started to develop self-awareness, I stopped seeing myself as a victim of my circumstances. Instead, I began to realize that my life's trajectory was in my hands, shaped by the choices I made every day. The beauty of self-awareness is that it gives you the clarity to recognize that while you can't always control the things that happen to you, you can control how you react to them. This realization was freeing. No longer did I need to wait for someone else to change my circumstances or wait for life to "become fair." I had the power to respond in ways that empowered me rather than trapped me.

How Self-Awareness Leads to Empowerment

The real power of self-awareness lies in choice. When you become aware of your thoughts, emotions, and behaviours, you can change them. Self-awareness allows you to interrupt automatic responses and take conscious control over how you engage with the world. This is a fundamental step in empowerment.

Rather than simply reacting to external situations, you start to choose how you want to respond. This empowers you to shape your own experience of the world. For example, instead of feeling victimized by difficult situations, you can shift your mindset and approach them with resilience, problem-solving, and positivity.

Studies by Dr. John Kabat-Zinn, the creator of Mindfulness-Based Stress Reduction (MBSR), have shown that mindfulness practices significantly improve emotional regulation and self-awareness, which are crucial for mental well-being and empowerment (*Kabat-Zinn, 1990*). Through regular mindfulness practice, we train our minds to be more present and aware, which enables us to better manage our emotions and responses.

The more you practice self-awareness, the stronger you'll become at mastering your emotions and reactions. You'll no longer be swayed by external factors like criticism, challenges, or judgment. You'll become anchored in your own self-awareness, knowing that your power lies in the choices you make, not in how others see you or treat you.

Practical Steps to Build Self-Awareness

Step 1: Observe Your Thoughts and Emotions

Start with a simple mindfulness practice. Set aside 5–10 minutes each day to check in with yourself. Find a quiet space, close your eyes, and focus on your breath. As thoughts and emotions arise, don't judge them. Just observe.

For example:

- Thought: "I'm not good enough."
- Emotion: "Frustration."

Instead of labelling these feelings, just say to yourself, *"I'm noticing that I'm feeling frustrated right now."*

This practice builds emotional awareness, helping you separate from your thoughts and feelings rather than being consumed by them. This allows you to make conscious choices instead of reacting automatically.

Step 2: Reflect on Your Reactions

After an emotional reaction, pause and reflect. Ask yourself:

- What triggered my emotional response?
- What beliefs or thoughts contributed to my reaction?
- How could I have responded differently?

- For instance, after receiving criticism from a colleague, instead of shutting down, reflect:

- *"I felt defensive because I fear judgment, a fear rooted in childhood experiences. I could have asked for clarity and remained open to feedback."*

This reflective exercise connects your emotions to deeper beliefs, helping you understand your reactions and respond with intention.

Step 3: Take Responsibility for Your Choices

Before reacting in any situation, pause for a moment. Consciously choose how you want to respond. This is especially important in stressful or emotionally charged moments.

Ask yourself:

- *What's the best way to respond?*
- *How do I want to show up in this situation?*

For example, if someone cuts you off in traffic, instead of reacting with anger, pause and choose to remain calm. This small moment of control shifts your emotional state and strengthens your empowerment.

Step into Your Power

You are not a passive observer of your life. You are the architect of your journey. When you recognize that you control your reactions and responses, you take back your power. The next time life challenges you, remember that you get to choose how you respond.

The moment you choose to observe your thoughts, reflect on your emotions, and consciously respond to the world, you'll realize that the life you've been waiting for is already within your grasp. You've always had the power.

Lesson 4

Forgiveness is Freedom

"Forgiveness isn't about them , it's about setting yourself free from the weight they left behind."

Forgiveness is one of the most powerful tools for personal growth. For years, I held onto anger, especially towards my father. I believed that my resentment was a shield, protecting me from future pain. In reality, it was a prison that kept me chained to my past. The truth is, forgiveness is not for the other person, it's for you. It's about releasing the emotional baggage and reclaiming your peace.

The Power of Forgiveness

Research shows that forgiveness has profound psychological and physical benefits. According to Dr. Everett Worthington (2001), forgiveness is an intentional decision to release feelings of resentment or vengeance toward someone who has harmed you. It is not about excusing the person's actions, but about letting go of the hold those actions have on your emotions and your future. When you choose to forgive, you liberate yourself, opening the door to personal growth and peace.

In my own life, I struggled with forgiving my father for years. I thought holding onto my anger protected me. But when I finally let go, I realized that forgiveness wasn't about excusing his behaviour, it was about freeing myself from the emotional weight I carried. As Dr. Frederic Luskin (2002) emphasizes in his book *Forgive for Good,* forgiveness allows you to "break the cycle" of resentment and bitterness, giving you the freedom to move forward.

The Cost of Holding onto Resentment

Carrying anger and resentment can have significant consequences. Studies show that prolonged resentment can lead to increased stress, anxiety, depression, and even physical illness.

Forgiving someone doesn’t change the past, but it transforms your future. When you hold onto resentment, you're allowing someone else’s actions to dictate your emotional state. By forgiving, you take back your power. Forgiveness isn’t about the person who hurt you, it’s about you regaining control over your emotional health.

Practical Steps for **Forgiveness**

1. Acknowledge Your Hurt

The first step toward forgiveness is acknowledging the hurt you feel. Many people try to suppress or avoid these painful emotions, but allowing yourself to fully feel and express your anger is crucial to healing. Journaling is a powerful tool for this.

- **Step 1**: Find a quiet space and take a few deep breaths to center yourself.

- **Step 2**: Write a letter to the person who hurt you, expressing your anger and pain. Don't hold back, let your emotions flow freely. Example: *"When you ignored my needs, it made me feel unimportant and abandoned."*

- **Step 3**: Once you've written the letter, tear it up or burn it as a symbolic gesture of letting go.

- This process of externalizing your emotions helps you process them and release their hold over you. Studies show that expressive writing can reduce emotional distress and improve mental health (Pennebaker, 1997).

2. *Let Go of the Need for Justice*

- Forgiveness is about letting go of the need for justice or revenge. It's not about excusing the actions that hurt you, but about choosing peace over bitterness. This can be difficult, especially if you feel that justice is deserved.

- **Step 1**: Take a deep breath and acknowledge your pain.

- **Step 2**: Practice an affirmation: *"I choose peace over resentment."*

- **Step 3**: Visualize yourself releasing anger and moving forward with peace. Imagine your heart lightening and your mind finding clarity.

3. ***Forgive Yourself First***

- Self-forgiveness is just as important as forgiving others. Many people struggle with self-blame or guilt, which can keep them from moving forward. Self-forgiveness is about recognizing your imperfections, taking responsibility for your mistakes, and choosing to grow from them.

- **Step 1**: Acknowledge any mistakes or regrets you have. For example, *"I made a poor decision, and I hurt someone I care about."*

- **Step 2**: Reflect on what you've learned from the experience. Ask yourself: *"What can I do differently next time?"*

- **Step 3**: Forgive yourself by saying: *"I forgive myself and choose to learn from this experience.*

Forgiveness is a gift you give to yourself, not the person who wronged you. By forgiving, you reclaim your peace and emotional freedom, allowing you to move forward and live a healthier, more fulfilled life. Forgiveness doesn't erase the past, but it transforms your future.

Lesson 5

Own Your Unique Journey

"Your journey is yours alone, shaped by trials only you've faced and victories only you've earned.

Your journey is uniquely yours,no one else has walked your exact path, faced your particular challenges, or achieved your specific victories. The power of this truth lies in the fact that your experiences, struggles, and successes are yours to own. Yet, in a world filled with social comparisons and filtered highlights of others' lives, it's easy to forget this.

I spent many years trapped in the comparison game, watching others seem to thrive while I was stuck in what felt like an endless cycle of struggle. I asked myself, why does it look so easy for them? Why do they seem to have it all together while I'm still working through the same challenges? But, with time, I came to realize something crucial, everyone has their own battles. The path you're walking may not look like anyone else's, and that's exactly how it's meant to be.

When I stopped measuring my progress against others, I finally found peace. My journey wasn't a race, and it wasn't about competing with anyone else. It was about understanding that every obstacle, every misstep, and every moment of frustration was shaping me into the person I was meant to become.

The act of comparison steals our joy, and that's where the real damage happens. We measure our worth against the perceived success of others, failing to appreciate how far we've come or how much we've grown. But once you embrace the idea that your path is uniquely yours, you unlock the power to thrive without needing anyone else's approval.

J.K. Rowling, The Power of Perseverance

Before *Harry Potter* became a global phenomenon, J.K. Rowling faced years of rejection. Her manuscript was turned down by multiple publishers, but rather than giving up or comparing her journey to the success of others, she stayed committed to her path. In a commencement speech at Harvard University, Rowling shared how comparison almost derailed her: *"It's impossible to live without failing at something, unless you live so cautiously that you might as well not have lived at all. In the end, failure is what made me stronger."* Rowling's journey teaches us that even setbacks, when embraced as part of your unique journey, become valuable lessons leading to success.

Practical Steps:

1. Celebrate Your Progress:

Every small win is a victory. It's easy to focus on what you haven't accomplished, but when you start recognizing your progress, no matter how small, you shift your mindset. Research by psychologist Dr. Shawn Achor in *The Happiness Advantage* emphasizes the importance of recognizing small achievements to build

long-term happiness and success.
Step 1: At the end of each day, jot down at least three things you accomplished. These don't have to be monumental, small victories count.
Example:"I got out of bed on time,""I completed a task at work," or "I connected with a friend."
Step 2: If you're struggling to think of wins, reflect on your effort, not just the outcome. Even if you didn't finish a project, acknowledge that you made progress. Celebrating progress not only reinforces positive behaviour but shifts your focus from scarcity to abundance, helping you appreciate where you are now.

2. Focus on Personal Milestones:

Stop comparing your growth to others. Instead, measure your progress against who you were yesterday. This keeps you grounded in your own journey and helps build long-term motivation.

Step 1: At the end of each week, ask yourself:

- "What did I achieve this week that I didn't last week?"
- "How did I handle challenges differently?"

Step 2: Write down your reflections, no matter how small. Acknowledge your progress.
Example: "This week, I set better boundaries with my time" or "I tried a new technique at work that paid off."
By focusing on your personal milestones, you'll recognize that your growth is not linear, and that's okay. Progress isn't about competing; it's about becoming.

3. Embrace Your Unique Struggles:

Comparing your struggles to others only creates self-doubt. Instead, focus on how your unique challenges have shaped you. In *The Gifts of Imperfection*, Dr. Brené Brown talks about the power of owning your imperfections, showing how they contribute to your personal growth.
Step 1: When you notice yourself comparing your journey to others, stop and remind yourself: *"My path is uniquely mine."*
Step 2: Affirm your individuality with statements like:

- "I am exactly where I need to be."
- "Every obstacle is helping me grow into who I'm meant to be."

Step 3: Journal about how your struggles have strengthened you. Reflect on your growth and how the challenges you've faced are integral to your story.
Example: "I've learned resilience in dealing with setbacks at work" or "My personal challenges have deepened my compassion for others."
Embrace your struggles as integral to your growth, recognizing that they are the very building blocks of your future success.

Your journey is uniquely yours, shaped by your experiences, challenges, and growth. The key to finding peace and fulfilment lies in embracing your path without comparing it to others. By celebrating small wins, focusing on personal milestones, and accepting the struggles that come your way, you'll build resilience and self-worth. Remember, there is no universal timeline for success, your progress is yours to own. Trust that every step, no matter how small, is moving you closer to the person you are meant to become. Embrace your journey with confidence and celebrate the beautiful, one-of-a-kind story you are creating.

Chapter Summary

In this chapter, we integrated the practical exercises from all five lessons to provide a holistic approach to personal growth. These exercises are designed to guide you through overcoming pain, building self-belief, developing self-awareness, and embracing your unique journey.

1. **Moving Through Pain**: Start by acknowledging your pain daily and reframing your perspective on challenges. Use journaling to reflect on your growth, building resilience through self-awareness of your emotional responses.

2. **Building Self-Belief**: Identify moments when you seek validation, and reaffirm your worth by creating a list of strengths. Engage in activities that don't rely on external approval to build intrinsic self-esteem.

3. **Self-Awareness**: Develop mindfulness by observing your thoughts and reactions, reflecting on triggers, and taking responsibility for your responses. These exercises encourage a deeper understanding of yourself and strengthen emotional control.

4. **Forgiveness**: Practice acknowledging your hurt, letting go of the need for justice, and forgiving both yourself and others. These steps help release emotional burdens, fostering peace and growth.

5. **Owning Your Unique Journey**: Celebrate every small win, focus on personal milestones, and embrace your struggles as vital to your growth. By acknowledging and accepting the uniqueness of your path, you empower yourself to move forward with confidence.

Together, these exercises create a powerful toolkit for personal transformation, guiding you toward a more resilient, self-aware, and fulfilled life. Trust your process, celebrate progress, and embrace every step of your journey.

Now that you've begun the process of healing, acknowledging your pain, and letting go of the past, it's time to take the next step: *Claiming Your Power and Rising Above.* In Chapter 2, we'll focus on building the confidence to stand firm in your worth, embrace your strength, and take ownership of your happiness. Healing sets the foundation, but true transformation happens when you rise into your power and live authentically. It's time to step into your greatness and claim the life you deserve.

Section: 2

Claiming your Power and Rising Above

I now proudly say that I am an optimistic person, but it wasn't always this way. My childhood was far from ideal. It was filled with physical and emotional punishments that lasted well into my teenage years, even when I was 21. My parents, especially my mother, believed in harsh discipline; beatings, yelling, and verbal abuse were daily occurrences. The thought process behind their actions was simple in their minds: strictness would keep us obedient. But the obedience they sought was not born of respect, but of fear.

Living in such an environment took its toll on my mental health. It shattered my self-esteem, stripped me of my confidence, and made me feel completely worthless. My mother's punishments were particularly severe. If I didn't comply with her demands, the consequences were harsh; objects thrown at me in anger, physical blows, and verbal assaults. The emotional impact of hearing those hurtful words daily was crushing. I felt unloved, unwanted, and often wished I could escape. The love a child is supposed to feel from their parents was absent in my home, replaced by fear and constant humiliation.

What made it even more painful was that I could never understand why I was treated this way. My sisters were subjected to the same punishments, but somehow, I bore the brunt of it. It felt like my parents were trying to break our spirits, to mould us into what they thought was the perfect obedient child, but all they succeeded in doing was creating a sense of fear in us. I wanted to run away, to find peace, to feel safe somewhere, but there was no place for that in my home.

As I grew older, particularly in my teenage years, I began to hate my parents for the way they treated me. It became even harder to reconcile the idea of love with the actions they showed me. They might have thought they were doing what was best, but for me, it was nothing more than emotional and psychological torture. The bitterness from their behaviour ran deep, and I couldn't escape it.

This deep emotional turmoil didn't stay confined to my home; it followed me into school. In the classroom, I felt like an outsider; detached, lost in my own world, and constantly disconnected from the people around me. I wasn't the typical bubbly, energetic child who thrived in the classroom. Instead, I became the quiet, withdrawn student who sat at the back of the class, staring blankly out of the window, my mind drifting far away from the lesson in front of me.

My teachers quickly noticed my behaviour and, concerned for my well-being, even spoke to my parents about it. I remember one teacher in particular suggesting that I might be dealing with depression, but at the time, I didn't even know what that meant. To me, I was just existing; numb, overwhelmed, and unable to focus on anything. I couldn't remember the last time I had laughed, or the last time I had cared about my grades. My mind was consumed with the weight of everything happening at home, and my schoolwork felt trivial in comparison.

It was hard to concentrate in class. When the teacher called my name, I would often be so zoned out that I couldn't even hear her. I wasn't failing on purpose; it was simply that my mind was elsewhere, lost in thoughts of the turmoil I faced at home. I didn't raise my hand, didn't engage in class discussions, and most of the time, I didn't even bother to do my assignments. I was just floating through the motions, disconnected from everyone and everything.

The isolation I felt at home seemed to follow me to school, and it wasn't just the teacher's concerns that weighed on me; it was the relentless teasing from my classmates. I was different. Quiet. Shy. People often picked up on that and used it to their advantage. The bullying started innocently enough, with whispers behind my back, but soon escalated into something far more painful.

There was one girl, in particular, who made my school life even more unbearable. She seemed to thrive on making me feel small, and she didn't hesitate to involve her friends in making my days miserable. They would taunt me in the hallways, call me names, and make jokes at my expense. The worst part was when they would mock my clothes, the way I carried myself, and my quiet demeanour. It was as if they knew exactly how to press my buttons and break me down further. I started to feel like there was something inherently wrong with me. I wasn't confident enough to stand up for myself, and so, I quietly accepted their cruel treatment.

But it wasn't just the taunts and the teasing. One day, during a winter break, the bullying escalated to a point that felt almost like a final straw. I was walking by the water taps when the girl and her friends approached me, laughing amongst them. Before I could react, they threw an entire bucket of freezing cold water on me. I stood there, drenched and shivering, as they laughed hysterically. My books were soaked, and the cold water burned my skin as it seeped into my clothes. The humiliation was unbearable. I was frozen, not just from the cold, but from the weight of my own shame. My classmates, watching from afar, snickered, some even joining in on the ridicule.

I had never been more humiliated in my life. But this time, something inside me snapped. Instead of silently retreating like I usually did, I found myself angry, more than I had ever been before. I couldn't stay quiet anymore. Without thinking, I turned around and slapped the girl across the face. She hit me back, but I didn't care. I felt something shifting within me, something I had never allowed myself to feel before: defiance.

At that moment, a teacher appeared on the scene, just as she always did whenever something went wrong. I expected her to scold me for reacting, but instead, she took me aside, away from the laughter and stares. She said something I will never forget: "No one will come to protect you, Simran. If you stay weak, people will continue to bully you for the rest of your life. People will change, but you'll keep getting abused unless you stand up for yourself. If you don't want that, you need to learn to defend yourself. I can protect you here, but not outside. So, stand up for yourself."

Those words were like a beacon of light cutting through the darkness that had been consuming me. They gave me the strength I didn't know I had. For the first time in my life, I realized I had a choice. I didn't have to keep accepting the abuse, the humiliation, and the helplessness. I could take control. That teacher's words were a turning point, a wake-up call that resonated deeply within me.

After that day, everything started to change. The bullying didn't stop overnight, but my reaction to it shifted completely. I no longer allowed myself to shrink away or hide in the shadows. I fought back; not just with physical actions, but with my newfound confidence. I began to stand up for myself, to assert my boundaries, and to hold my head up high. It wasn't easy, and there were days when I felt vulnerable, but I pushed through. I knew I couldn't go back to the person I was before.

By the time I moved to a new school, my personality had already begun to evolve. I no longer saw myself as a victim. The change was evident. I became more outgoing, more assertive, and less afraid to show who I truly was. I stopped worrying about what others thought of me. I began to focus on my own growth, on building my confidence and pursuing my dreams, despite the obstacles.

Academically, I started excelling. I didn't just want to pass; I wanted to prove to myself that I could achieve greatness, that my past would not define my future. The shift in my mindset was palpable. I wasn't just getting good grades to please others or to avoid punishment; I was doing it for me. By the time I reached my final exams, I had gone from barely scraping by to scoring 84%. More than the grades, it was the knowledge that I had overcome my inner struggles that gave me the most satisfaction.

This transformation wasn't just about academic success. It was about becoming someone I could be proud of. The girl who had once been quiet and fearful was now the woman who stood strong in the face of adversity, who refused to let anyone dim her light. I was no longer the person my past had tried to make me. I was someone new; someone who knew her worth, who had learned to fight for herself, and who was determined to continue growing.

And I haven't looked back since. Every step I take now is driven by the strength and confidence I found within myself. The journey is far from over, but every day is a testament to the fact that I can overcome anything, no matter how dark the past might have been.

The Moment I Took Control:

As I reflect on my journey, I realize that everything I went through was not just a series of unfortunate events, but a necessary process of growth. Every moment of pain, every tear, every time I was made to feel small, contributed to the person I am today. The journey wasn't easy, and there were days when I felt like giving up, when the weight of my past seemed too heavy to carry. But each setback became a stepping stone that taught me valuable lessons.

It wasn't the physical abuse or the bullying that broke me; it was the belief I had in myself that had been broken. But here's the thing I learned: you are not defined by what happens to you. The way others treat you, the circumstances you face; they don't determine who you are. What matters is how you respond, how you rise from those difficult moments, and how you use your pain to fuel your growth.

There was a turning point in my life, a moment when I realized that I couldn't keep waiting for someone to rescue me, to change my circumstances for me. I had to take control. I had to take responsibility for my own happiness, my own success, and my own future. The true power lies within us to rise above adversity, to turn our struggles into strength.

And that is the essence of true transformation. It's about believing that you are worthy, that your past does not dictate your future, and that no matter how dark the road gets, there is always light ahead; if you are willing to fight for it.

Lesson 6

You Are Stronger Than You Think

"Within you lies a strength you've yet to fully meet"

When we think of strength, most of us picture someone lifting heavy weights or completing a gruelling physical challenge. But real strength? It's not about the muscles. It's about character, resilience, and the ability to keep going when life pushes back hard. True strength emerges from adversity, and every challenge is an opportunity to build that strength.

Nelson Mandela's 27 Years in Prison:
Nelson Mandela's life is a perfect example of how adversity builds true strength. Spending 27 years in prison for fighting against apartheid didn't break him, it forged him. Mandela's perseverance, despite unimaginable hardship, led him to become South Africa's first Black president. His journey exemplifies the transformative power of resilience.

Psychologist Carol Dweck's concept of a growth mindset explains why some people thrive in the face of challenges. Those who embrace struggle as an opportunity to learn and grow are more likely to succeed in the long run. This mindset isn't just about intelligence, it's about perseverance and how you approach setbacks.

Thomas Edison's "Failures"

Thomas Edison didn't just create the lightbulb on his first try. In fact, he famously went through 1,000 failures before he succeeded. Yet, he didn't view these setbacks as failures, each one was simply a step closer to his goal. His story teaches us that the obstacles we face are stepping stones to our greatest achievements.

True strength doesn't always appear in a flashy way. It's not about how tough you look on the outside. It's about the inner strength that keeps you moving forward when everything seems impossible. Resilience is about getting back up after life knocks you down. Even when you didn't feel strong, you were. Every time you faced hardship and chose to keep going, you were proving your strength.

Studies show that people often emerge stronger after trauma. They report increased personal strength, a deeper appreciation for life, and a greater sense of purpose. This reinforces the idea that challenges aren't meant to break us, they help us grow into the people we were always meant to be.

Malala Yousafzai's Resilience

Malala Yousafzai was shot by the Taliban for advocating girls' education. Despite this traumatic event, she didn't retreat into fear. Instead, she became a global advocate for education and women's rights. Her recovery and activism show how trauma can be the catalyst for extraordinary strength and purpose.

Practical Steps:

1. Recognize Your Inner Power

- Reflect on past challenges where you showed resilience.
  Example: Think of a tough time. What inner strength did you tap into to overcome it?
- Write down affirmations based on your past victories. When overwhelmed, remind yourself of your strength by revisiting these affirmations.

2. Cultivate a Mindset of Perseverance

- Choose a mantra that encourages you to keep going: "Every setback is a setup for a comeback."
- Place your mantra somewhere visible.
- In tough times, repeat your mantra to yourself. Reflect on how it helped you persevere and move forward.

3. Take Small, Consistent Steps

- Break down your larger goals into smaller tasks.
- Track your daily progress. Whether it's a fitness goal, writing a book, or improving your career.
- Reflect weekly on the small steps you've taken and how they're bringing you closer to your goal.

Strength isn't a one-time achievement; it's a lifelong journey. Every challenge you face will make you stronger, more resilient, and better equipped for the future. You've already proven you can handle so much more than you think. Embrace each challenge, knowing that every struggle is another opportunity to discover just how strong you really are.

Lesson 7

Stand Up For Yourself – Take Ownership of Your Worth

"When you stand up for yourself, you declare your worth to the world"

Standing up for yourself isn't just about defending your actions in a moment of conflict; it's about embracing your value unapologetically and taking ownership of your worth in all areas of your life. It's about claiming your space in the world and setting the tone for how you deserve to be treated, by others and by yourself.

Research has shown that when we stand up for ourselves, not only do we strengthen our self-esteem, but we also encourage others to treat us with greater respect.

The Power of Boundaries

Setting boundaries is one of the most important ways to protect your emotional well-being. It's about respecting your own needs and establishing limits that allow you to thrive. Individuals with clear personal boundaries are more likely to experience higher levels of psychological well-being and satisfaction in relationships.

Dr. Brené Brown, a research professor at the University of Houston and a widely respected author on vulnerability and self-worth, emphasizes the importance of boundaries in maintaining emotional health. In her TED Talk, "The Power of Vulnerability," Brown shares how vulnerability is a strength, but boundaries are crucial to prevent burnout and protect your worth. She advocates for the idea that you don't have to say "yes" to everything in order to be loved or respected. Setting boundaries, she argues, is not about being rude; it's about protecting your emotional space.

Brown's own experience, as she openly discusses in her books, shows that even as a highly successful researcher, she has had to draw lines with her time and energy. Her willingness to set boundaries helped her maintain her mental health and continue to create meaningful work without losing herself in the process.

Taking Control of How Others Treat You

When you stand up for yourself, you set the tone for how others treat you. Individuals who assert themselves tend to experience healthier relationships, with fewer instances of mistreatment or disrespect. The act of setting boundaries and standing firm in your values is a clear message to others: you are worthy of respect.

The Case of Maya Angelou

Maya Angelou, the celebrated author and civil rights activist, provides an inspiring real-life example of standing up for oneself and asserting worth. In her autobiography, *I Know Why the Caged Bird Sings*, Angelou reflects on how, despite facing numerous challenges and racial discrimination, she found her voice and the courage to speak out for herself. One powerful instance was when she decided not to tolerate any mistreatment in her relationships, both personal and professional. Angelou's refusal to accept disrespect, coupled with her strong sense of self, allowed her to navigate even the toughest situations with grace and strength. Her example demonstrates how standing up for your worth can create space for authentic relationships based on mutual respect.

It's Not Arrogance, It's Self-Respect

A common misconception is that standing up for you is a form of arrogance. However, self-respect is not about putting others down, it's about honoring your own value. People who have high self-respect tend to have better emotional stability, stronger relationships, and higher levels of personal fulfilment.

The Case of Oprah Winfrey

Oprah Winfrey, one of the most influential women in media, is a great example of someone who has never allowed arrogance to overshadow her sense of self-worth. Oprah is known for her boundary-setting and refusal to compromise on her values. In an interview with *Harvard Business Review*, she spoke about how, early in her career, she had to stand up for herself in the face of discrimination and unfair treatment. One turning point in her career was when she decided to quit a job that no longer aligned with her values. Oprah's self-respect wasn't about arrogance; it was about understanding her worth and not settling for less than she deserved.

When you stand up for yourself, you build confidence. The process of asserting your worth, whether by setting boundaries or speaking up in tough situations, reinforces your belief in your abilities.

The Case of Serena Williams

Serena Williams, one of the greatest tennis players of all time, is another powerful example of standing up for your worth and building confidence. Williams has been vocal about the challenges she has faced as a Black woman in a predominantly white sport. Throughout her career, she has had to assert her worth, particularly when faced with criticism or unjust treatment from the media. In a 2018 interview with *Vogue,* Williams spoke about how standing up for herself,whether in business negotiations or on the tennis court,helped her gain respect and confidence. She recognizes that each time she asserts her value, it strengthens her self-belief. Her journey shows that confidence is built through consistent self-assertion and the refusal to accept disrespect.

Practical Steps for Standing Up For Yourself

1. **Define Your Worth**

Step 1: Reflect on your core strengths and unique qualities. What are your proudest accomplishments?

Step 2: Write down your personal and professional achievements, and create a list of qualities that define your value.

Step 3: Revisit this list regularly to remind yourself of your worth and the unique contributions you bring to the world.

2. **Practice Self-Affirmation**

Step 1: Choose 3-5 affirmations that resonate with your self-worth. These should be positive, empowering statements such as: "I am worthy of respect and kindness," or "My value is inherent."

Step 2: Say these affirmations aloud each morning and night. Stand tall and speak with confidence.

Step 3: Keep a journal of your thoughts and any shifts in your belief about your worth.

3. **Set Boundaries**

Step 1: Identify areas in your life where you feel disrespected or taken for granted. These could be in work, relationships, or social settings.

Step 2: Write down specific boundaries you want to set to protect your time, energy, and mental well-being.

Step 3: Start asserting these boundaries in small ways, saying no when necessary, redirecting conversations, or protecting your personal time.

Step 4: Enforce these boundaries consistently and lovingly. If others push back, remind them of your needs and reaffirm your worth.

Standing up for yourself is a powerful act of self-respect and a foundational step toward cultivating a life of confidence and fulfilment. Whether it's through setting boundaries, asserting your worth, or practicing self-affirmation, every time you stand firm in your value, you build the confidence to navigate challenges and relationships with authenticity. Remember, when you take ownership of your worth, you inspire others to do the same.

Lesson 8

Your Past Doesn't Define You

"Your past is a chapter, not the whole story"

Your past is one chapter in the greater book of your life. Too often, we're tempted to define ourselves based on our past mistakes, regrets, or missed opportunities. We can get stuck in these memories, as if they're the entire story of who we are. But the truth is, your past doesn't determine your future, it's just one part of your journey, and you hold the pen to write the rest.

If you've experienced hardships, failures, or regrets, know that these challenges have shaped you, but they do not have the power to define your entire life. The beauty of life is that we always have the chance to rewrite our future. A chapter doesn't define the entire book. The most empowering realization is that you are the author of your own story, and you can create new chapters at any time.

Steve Jobs' Comeback

Consider Steve Jobs, the co-founder of Apple. In 1985, after facing a highly publicized ousting from his own company, he could have let that failure define him. Instead, he went on to create Pixar and NeXT, and returned to Apple to lead it to unprecedented success. His story is one of resilience. He didn't let the failures of the past dictate his future. Jobs turned rejection into an opportunity to innovate, and when he returned to Apple, he led the company into a new era of technology with groundbreaking products like the iPod, iPhone, and iPad.

Steve Jobs' life story is a powerful reminder that your past doesn't define who you are or where you're going. If you're willing to learn from your failures and keep moving forward, there is no limit to what you can achieve.

The Role of Your Past in Shaping Your Future

It's important to recognize that while your past has shaped you, it doesn't define you. The events, struggles, and mistakes of your past are all part of the process, but they are not the destination. They are moments that teach you, that build your resilience, and ultimately prepare you for the next chapter.

Research Insight: The Science of Self-Forgiveness

Psychological research supports this notion. Self-forgiveness is strongly correlated with emotional well-being. When you let go of your past mistakes, you free yourself from the burden of guilt, regret, and shame. By practicing self-forgiveness, you can move on with greater emotional freedom, allowing you to fully embrace the present and future.

Letting go of past mistakes doesn't mean forgetting or erasing them. It means acknowledging them as part of your journey and choosing not to let them control your present or future. When you forgive yourself, you allow space for growth and new possibilities. Your past does not determine your value or worth; your future is what you make of it.

The Future: Unwritten and Full of Possibility

You are not defined by your past. While it has shaped you, it doesn't dictate your future. The future is unwritten, and every choice you make today is a step toward the life you desire. Whether you're pursuing a new goal, learning from past mistakes, or simply choosing to believe in your potential, every action you take today is an investment in your future.

Practical Steps to Empower Yourself

1. Let Go of Past Mistakes

- **Step 1:** Write down a past mistake causing emotional pain.
- **Step 2:** Identify the lesson learned from this experience.
- **Step 3:** Remind yourself that the mistake doesn't define you.
- **Step 4:** Write a letter forgiving yourself.
- **Step 5:** Symbolically release the mistake (tear up the paper, burn it, etc.).

This exercise helps you shift from regret to growth, freeing you to move forward.

2. Focus on the Present

- **Step 1:** Choose a mindful activity (eating, walking, breathing).

- **Step 2:** Engage fully with your senses during this activity.
- **Step 3:** If your mind wanders, gently bring your focus back.
- **Step 4:** Journal about how it felt to be fully present.

This practice helps ground you in the present moment, reducing anxiety and enhancing decision-making.

3. Create a New Narrative

- **Step 1:** Write down your current personal story.
- **Step 2:** Reflect on past moments where you overcame challenges.
- **Step 3:** Rewrite your story, focusing on your strengths and growth.
- **Step 4:** Visualize your future story and write it down.
- **Step 5:** Read your new narrative aloud daily.

Your past may have been challenging, but it doesn't have to dictate your future. The future is unwritten, and it's yours to create. You have the power to move beyond your past mistakes and transform your life with every decision you make.

Lesson 09

Your Voice Is Your Strength – Don't Let Anyone Silence You

"Your voice holds your power, truth, and identity."

Your voice is your superpower. It is the foundation of your identity, the tool you use to assert your needs, and the way you express who you are to the world. When you speak up, you not only communicate your thoughts but also affirm your existence, declare your worth, and empower others to do the same. This lesson will guide you to reclaim the power of your voice and use it to create meaningful change in your life and the world around you.

Your voice carries more weight than you may realize. It's a vehicle for expressing your boundaries, your needs, and your dreams. When you speak up, you don't just make your needs known, you also inspire others to do the same. By using your voice, you send a message that your opinions matter, that your experiences are valid, and that your voice will not be silenced.

Don't Let Fear or Doubt Stop You

Fear is one of the greatest barriers to speaking up. We fear judgment, rejection, and misunderstanding, which often causes us to remain silent. But your voice is not about perfection, it's about courage. Even if your voice shakes or you feel unsure, what matters is that you speak anyway. When you allow fear or doubt to control your voice, you give up your power. Speaking up, even in small ways, can gradually break that barrier.

According to a study, women often fear speaking up in professional environments due to the potential for judgment. However, research shows that those who push past that fear are viewed as more confident and more likely to receive promotions. This shows that speaking up, despite fear, can elevate your career and self-esteem.

No One Can Dim Your Light

There will always be people who try to silence you, whether through interruptions, dismissiveness, or even outright criticism. But remember: when you stop speaking, you give others the power to define your reality. No one can dim your light unless you let them. Your voice reflects your inner strength, and it has the power to push through even the harshest challenges.

Practical Step: The next time someone interrupts or dismisses you, calmly but firmly say, "I wasn't finished speaking," and continue your point. This small act reaffirms your right to be heard.

Every Expression Matters – Whether Big or Small

It's easy to assume that only grand gestures or bold declarations count as self-expression, but every small act of speaking up matters. Whether you're sharing your opinion in a meeting, expressing a need to a friend, or asking for help, each instance of self-expression is a way to reclaim your power. These small moments add up over time, creating a ripple effect that strengthens your confidence.

Rosa Parks' quiet refusal to give up her seat sparked the civil rights movement. It wasn't a loud speech or a dramatic protest; it was a small act of resistance that led to massive social change. Your voice, no matter how small the act, has the potential to create change (Parks, 1992).

Your Voice Is a Tool for Change

Your voice is not just a way to express yourself, it is also a tool for creating change. When you speak up about injustice, challenge the status quo, or advocate for what you believe in, you are actively shaping the world around you. Your words have the power to influence and inspire others, sparking movements and initiating change.

Practical Steps to Empower Your Voice

1. Speak Your Truth

- **Task:** Write down your thoughts, feelings, and desires. Reflect on what you've been holding back and why. Practice speaking your truth out loud to a trusted friend or in front of a mirror.

- **Goal:** This will help you become more comfortable with vocalizing your feelings and thoughts in different contexts.

2. Stand Up for Others

- **Task:** Identify a person in your life who could benefit from your support. Speak up for them, whether it's in a professional setting, among friends, or within your community.

- **Goal:** By standing up for others, you also build your own confidence and assertiveness.

3. Be Unapologetic

- **Task:** Create a list of affirmations that reflect your unapologetic stance. Start each day by stating these affirmations out loud and visualize yourself living unapologetically.

- **Goal:** By affirming your value and voice, you will slowly break the habit of shrinking or apologizing unnecessarily.

Your voice is powerful. It is a tool for setting boundaries, creating change, and empowering yourself and others. Don't let fear, doubt, or external pressures silence you. Each time you speak up, whether in big or small ways, you claim your power and affirm your value. When you speak your truth, you inspire others to do the same, creating a ripple effect that leads to personal transformation and collective empowerment. Your voice matters. Use it to change your life and the world around you.

Lesson 10

You Deserve to Be Happy – Make It a Priority

"Happiness isn't a luxury, it's your right."

Happiness isn't a luxury or something you earn after you achieve certain goals. It's your right, right here, right now. Too often, we believe happiness is something we can only experience once we've ticked off a long list of achievements, a new job, a relationship, a perfect body. But the truth is, happiness is a choice you can make today.

Research shows that about 40% of our happiness is in our hands, determined by what we think, feel, and do on a daily basis. So, you don't have to wait for a "perfect" moment. You deserve happiness right now, and you can create it in the small moments of your everyday life.

Happiness Is Found in the Little Things

Most people think happiness comes from big milestones, landing that dream job or getting the perfect relationship. But the truth is, happiness doesn't wait for the "big stuff." It's in the little moments, your morning coffee, a hug from a friend, the sun on your face.

One of the longest studies on happiness, conducted over 80 years, revealed that strong relationships and moments of connection are far more important than career success or wealth. Meaningful relationships and small, shared joys are the true sources of happiness. When you embrace these everyday moments, you open yourself up to consistent joy.

Make Happiness a Priority, Not an Afterthought

Many of us push happiness to the side, thinking it will come later, after we've crossed off everything else on our to-do list. But here's the truth: when we neglect happiness for too long, we start feeling drained, disconnected, and overwhelmed.

Making your happiness a priority doesn't mean being selfish, it means taking care of yourself so you can show up for others in a better way. It's about investing time in what nourishes you, whether that's a hobby, a walk in nature, or just sitting quietly to breathe. Prioritizing your joy isn't optional. It's necessary.

Choose to Be Happy Now

We often think we'll be happy "later," after we've done more or reached certain goals. But happiness isn't something to put on hold. It's a mindset, a choice you can make right now, even in the middle of challenges.

Yes, life is tough sometimes. But research has shown that focusing on the positive, even small things, helps rewire your brain to find joy, even in difficult situations. Choosing happiness in the present moment doesn't mean ignoring your problems, it means acknowledging the good alongside the struggles.

Don't Wait for Permission to Be Happy

So often, we wait for permission to be happy. Maybe we think we haven't "earned" it yet, or we feel guilty for taking time to care for ourselves. But here's the deal: you don't need anyone's permission to feel joy. You are the only person who can decide when it's your time to be happy.

Stop waiting for the perfect moment or for others to give you the green light. You have the power to choose joy right now. No excuses.

Happiness Is a Practice

Just like any other skill, happiness requires practice. You don't wake up one day and suddenly feel perfectly happy, it takes intentional actions and habits that nurture your well-being. And the more you practice these habits, the easier it gets.

Studies show that practicing gratitude, mindfulness, and positive thinking can help you cultivate a deeper sense of happiness. The more you engage in these practices, the more you start to naturally shift your mindset toward joy.

Practical Steps to Cultivate Happiness

1. **Seek Moments of Joy Daily**
   Action: Every day, identify three things that brought you joy, no matter how small. Write them down in a Joy Journal. This helps you shift your focus to the

positive, increasing your sense of happiness over time.

2. **Let go of the "Someday" Mindset**
   Action: Choose one thing you've been postponing, and take a small step toward it today. Don't wait for the perfect conditions, start now, no matter how tiny the step.

3. **Prioritize Your Happiness**
   Action: Set aside time each day for something that brings you joy, whether it's a hobby, spending time with loved ones, or simply relaxing. Make happiness a non-negotiable part of your routine.

Happiness isn't something that comes *later*; it's available to you *right now*. Every small moment of joy you choose to acknowledge makes a difference. And by practicing gratitude, focusing on relationships, and carving out time for what makes you happy, you can create a more joyful life today.

You deserve happiness, not someday, but today. It's already within your reach, you just have to claim it.

Chapter Summary

In this chapter, we integrated the practical exercises from Lessons 6 to 10 to help you step into your power, embrace happiness, and use your voice to create meaningful change. These exercises are designed to guide you through the process of building confidence, expressing yourself authentically, and reclaiming your inner strength.

1. **Transforming Your Inner Dialogue:** Start by replacing negative self-talk with affirmations that reinforce your worth. Journaling and reflecting on your successes help reframe your mindset, turning self-doubt into self-belief.
2. **Expressing Your Voice with Confidence:** Practice speaking up in situations where the stakes are low, gradually building your assertiveness. Reaffirm your boundaries and use your voice to express your needs, ensuring your presence is felt in every space.
3. **Choosing Happiness in the Moment:** Engage in daily exercises that focus on identifying moments of joy, practicing gratitude, and letting go of the "someday" mindset. Make happiness a non-negotiable part of your daily life.
4. **Embracing Self-Expression:** Celebrate every act of self-expression, big or small. Whether it's asserting yourself in a meeting or supporting someone else, each expression of your truth builds momentum and strengthens your confidence.
5. **Owning Your Personal Power:** Reclaim the strength of your voice, even in the face of fear or doubt. Practice using your voice to challenge the status quo

and speak out for change, knowing that your words have the power to inspire and influence.

Together, these exercises create a powerful foundation for reclaiming your voice, embracing happiness, and stepping into your true power. By practicing these steps, you are building a confident, authentic, and empowered version of yourself that cannot be silenced.

Now that you've begun the process of cultivating a positive mindset, asserting your voice, and embracing joy, it's time to take the next step: Taking Control of Your Thoughts and Actions. In Chapter 3, we'll dive deeper into harnessing the power of positive thinking, taking meaningful action, and surrounding yourself with influences that nurture your growth. It's time to take your thoughts and actions to the next level to create lasting change in your life and the world around you.

Section: 3

A Life-Changing Encounter

After completing my 12th standard, Meira (my best friend) and I felt the urge to explore something new. We had always been passionate about books and knowledge, ever since childhood. Our love for reading had shaped much of who we were, and we knew we wanted to continue learning even after school. That's when we decided to join the district library, hoping to expand our horizons and discover new ideas.

That was the first time we met Librarian Sir, the head librarian. As soon as we walked into his office in the library, I felt something different. I've always been a bit intuitive, able to sense a person's energy; whether negative or positive. But with Librarian Sir, it was unlike anything I'd ever experienced before. He had an aura of calmness that I couldn't describe. His voice was soft yet reassuring, his demeanor so peaceful that it could calm the most troubled soul. He spoke to us with such patience, and I could feel the positivity radiating from him. We got our memberships and left the library that day deeply impressed by him.

Over the next few months, my best friend and I would visit the library regularly. Our initial conversations with Librarian Sir were about our studies and career goals, but soon, we became good friends. I began to confide in him about my personal struggles. At that time, I was going through a lot of emotional turmoil, especially with my family. I was quiet, tense, and rarely smiled. I didn't know how to deal with the chaos in my life, and Librarian Sir noticed this.

One day, after hearing my complaints about my family, he simply smiled and asked me, "Simran, is that it?" I was taken back. How could he not understand the gravity of what I was saying? Why was he so calm when everything around me seemed like a storm? He didn't offer any advice at that moment, but instead, he asked me to take a deep breath, drink some water, and relax. Then, he gave me a book; a motivational one; 'You can Win' Written by Shiv Khera, and told me to read it twice. He said, "When you come back next time, bring the book with you, and we'll talk about it."

I was disappointed. I had just opened up to him about my life, and he gave me a book instead of offering a solution. But despite my frustration, I was determined to follow his advice. I read that book with all the focus I could muster. And something extraordinary happened. As I read the book, I realized that it was saying exactly what Librarian Sir had been telling me all along. It spoke about the importance of controlling your thoughts, maintaining a positive mindset, and believing in the power of gratitude. In those pages, I saw the lessons I had been too stubborn to fully understand before.

The next time I visited Librarian Sir, he didn't ask me any questions about the book. He didn't need to. The change in me was visible. I was calmer, more positive, and less affected by the negativity around me. Librarian Sir could see it in my face. He didn't need to test me; the transformation was clear. He simply smiled, pleased that I had embraced the wisdom from the book, and continued to teach me the principles of gratitude, positive affirmation, and spirituality.

It didn't happen overnight, though. The change in me was gradual. Librarian Sir's words; though simple; started to make sense over time. The more I practiced gratitude and focused on the good things in my life, the more I noticed a shift in my mindset. I learned not to dwell on what my family was doing wrong, but to appreciate the people who supported me, like my best friend, who always brought joy into my life despite her quirks.

Eventually, I realized that life isn't about waiting for circumstances to change; it's about changing your perspective. Librarian Sir's teachings became my guiding light. I came to understand that our thoughts shape our reality. If we focus on the positive, we attract more good things into our lives. But if we dwell on negativity, we create our own suffering.

Librarian Sir didn't just help me find peace; he taught me to believe in myself and the power of positive thinking. He never asked for anything in return, but his support meant the world to me. His quiet guidance, his patience, and his unwavering belief in my potential had a profound impact on my life.

Looking back, I realize how fortunate I am to have crossed paths with someone like Librarian Sir. He was more than just a librarian; he was a mentor, a friend, and a life-changing influence. His advice didn't come in grand gestures or complicated solutions; it came in simple, profound words that continue to guide me to this day.

I will never be able to fully thank Librarian Sir for everything he has done for me. His influence has shaped me into the person I am today, and I carry his teachings with me every day. His words continue to resonate within me, and I've learned that life is all about the way we choose to think. If your thoughts are positive, your life will reflect that positivity.

I believe that when your intentions are pure and your heart is open, the universe will bring the right people into your life. Librarian Sir was one of those people for me. I will forever be grateful for his guidance and for the positive impact he has had on my life. He is like a godfather to me, and I will always keep him close in my heart.

Lesson 11

Take Control of Your Thoughts – The Power to Shape Your Reality

"Master your mind and you master your world. Your thoughts are the architects of your reality."

For much of my life, external circumstances, stress from work, family struggles, societal expectations, controlled my emotions. I allowed these influences to dictate my mental state, until I learned a profound truth: I have the power to control my thoughts.

This lesson is about realizing that thoughts are not facts. Negative thoughts, while inevitable, don't have to rule your life. You can choose how to respond to them. It's not about suppressing the negativity but about redirecting your focus to thoughts that empower you. The more you practice this, the more you'll see your emotional and mental state shift.

The Power of Your Mind

Your mind is a tool; you are its master, not the other way around. When you start to consciously take control of your thoughts, you shift your inner world. This, in turn, influences your outer world, helping you navigate challenges with a more grounded perspective.

Negative thoughts can snowball, especially when we feed into them. But just as you wouldn't continue to water a wilting plant, you don't have to nurture negative thinking. The key is to catch these thoughts early and redirect them toward positivity. It's a practice, one that requires patience and consistency, but the payoff is huge.

The more you practice focusing on the positive, the more it becomes second nature. It's not about ignoring your problems but learning how to respond to them with a mindset that supports your well-being.

Practical Steps to Take Control of Your Thoughts:

1. **Identify Negative Thought Patterns**
   Action: Start by observing your thoughts throughout the day. When negative or self-defeating thoughts arise, acknowledge them without judgment.
   Goal: Awareness is the first step to change. When you can spot a negative thought, you can choose to challenge it.

2. **Challenge and Replace Negative Thoughts**
   Action: Ask yourself: "Is this thought true?" and "Is this thought helpful?" Replace negative thoughts with empowering affirmations or constructive thoughts. For example, replace "I'll never succeed" with "I am capable, and I have the skills to succeed."
   Goal: Shift your mindset from self-limiting beliefs to self-empowering ones.

3. **Create a Ritual for Positivity**
   Action: Set aside a few minutes each day to practice

gratitude or affirmations. Use this time to focus your thoughts on the positive aspects of your life, no matter how small.
Goal: Reinforce positivity as a daily habit, making it easier to redirect your thoughts when negativity arises.

The Ripple Effect of Positive Thinking:

Redirecting your thoughts is a skill, and like any skill, the more you practice it, the easier it becomes. Over time, you'll notice a ripple effect, your emotional state will stabilize, your stress levels will decrease, and you'll feel more in control of your life. The benefits are not just mental; they extend to your actions, your relationships, and your overall sense of well-being.

Remember, this is not about perfection. You will still have negative thoughts, but you have the power to choose how to respond. Every time you choose positivity over negativity, you strengthen your ability to control your mind. This small act of choice, repeated consistently, is what creates lasting change.

Lesson 12

Take Action – The Bridge between Where You Are and Where You Want to Be

"Action is the bridge that turns dreams into destinations"

One of the most powerful lessons I learned from Librarian Sir was about taking action. For years, I was trapped in the cycle of over thinking, hoping for change without ever actually doing anything about it. I had big goals, but I often felt overwhelmed, unsure of where to start, or what the first step should be. That's when Librarian Sir gave me the simple but powerful lesson: Knowledge is not enough; action is what turns knowledge into change.

This lesson became the turning point in my life. The moment Librarian Sir handed me the book, it wasn't just about reading, it was about stepping into action. I was no longer a passive observer; I was now responsible for my transformation. It's easy to talk about change or think about it, but nothing happens until we **take action**.

The Power of Taking Action:

Often, we wait for the "perfect" moment or the ideal circumstances before we make a move. But the truth is, there will never be a perfect time. Taking action is about making the most of the present moment, no matter how small or imperfect it may seem.

Change doesn't happen overnight. It's the small, consistent actions that build momentum over time and lead to lasting transformation. Action is the catalyst that turns dreams into reality, whether it's taking a single step toward a goal or making a daily commitment to change.

James Clear – The Power of Small Habits:

James Clear, author of *Atomic Habits*, talks about the idea of "aggregation of marginal gains." In his approach, small, consistent actions, like reading a chapter each day or working out for just 15 minutes, compound over time to produce massive results. Clear's concept shows that even small actions, done consistently, can lead to extraordinary changes.

When people are stuck, they often think that they need drastic measures to get unstuck. But Clear's research shows that it's not about radical change; it's about the tiny, seemingly insignificant steps we take every day that ultimately drive us forward. Every action, no matter how small, adds up over time.

The Role of Action in Overcoming Fear and Procrastination:

The fear of failure and the uncertainty about the future often keep us paralyzed. Many people wait for the "perfect" plan before taking any steps. But, as I discovered, waiting for everything to be perfect is often just a form of procrastination. The key is to take that first step, no matter how small. In my own journey, the act of reading that book wasn't just about gaining knowledge; it was about deciding to engage in my own growth.

Action builds confidence. The more you act, the more you prove to yourself that you have the ability to create change. The more you step out of your comfort zone, the more momentum you build.

Practical Steps to Take Action:

1. **Break Goals Down:**
   Action: Large goals can feel overwhelming. Break them into smaller, manageable steps.
   Goal: This makes your objectives feel achievable, and every small win gives you the momentum to keep going.
2. **Take Immediate Action:**
   Action: Don't wait for the "right time." Start today with the smallest possible step, even if it's just one phone call or sending one email.
   Goal: Taking that first step is the hardest but most important part. Even the smallest action starts the momentum you need.
3. **Celebrate Progress:**
   Action: Acknowledge every small success, no matter how insignificant it may seem.
   Goal: Celebrating progress keeps you motivated and reinforces the habit of taking action.

Mel Robbins – The 5-Second Rule:

Mel Robbins, a motivational speaker and author, created the *5-Second Rule* to help people overcome hesitation and take action. The idea is simple: When you feel the urge to do something, you have five seconds to act before your mind talks you out of it. This rule is designed to help you take immediate action, bypassing self-doubt and hesitation.

Mel's case shows us that action doesn't require perfection; it requires courage to act despite fear. This principle is foundational to overcoming procrastination. By taking the first step, we shut down the mental resistance and build momentum.

The Bridge Between Where You Are and Where You Want to Be:

Action is the bridge that connects where you are now to where you want to be. It's easy to get stuck in the thinking phase, but without action, all that thinking remains theoretical. Action is what transforms intention into reality.

The lesson Librarian Sir taught me was that by taking action, we actively create our own future. It's through consistent, deliberate steps that we break free from old habits, limiting beliefs, and the comfort zone that keeps us stuck.

Inaction is the true enemy of progress. Every small action you take, no matter how imperfect, brings you closer to the life you envision. Whether it's reading a book, making that tough phone call, or simply deciding to start, each action is a step toward the transformation you desire. Take control of your journey by taking action today.

Now that you've taken the first step in reclaiming your thoughts and mindset, it's time to shift into high gear. In the next chapter, we'll explore how to embrace life's lessons, even when they're hard, and how every challenge is an opportunity for growth. The work you've done so far has prepared you for the next level, let's dive in!

Lesson 13

Surround Yourself with Positive Influences

"The energy around you shapes the energy within you; choose your circle wisely, and watch yourself thrive."

One of the most profound lessons I learned from Librarian Sir was the power of the people we surround ourselves with. Whether family, friends, colleagues, or mentors, the influence of those around us shapes our mindset, behaviour, and outlook on life. Librarian Sir was a prime example of this. His calm demeanour, unwavering positivity, and constructive energy created an environment where I felt encouraged and motivated to grow. He didn't just teach me through words, but by example, his life was the manifestation of the positivity and energy that I now aim to bring into my own life.

In today's fast-paced world, negativity can easily consume us. Whether from the media, personal struggles, or the people around us, it can drain our mental energy and keep us stuck. But what Librarian Sir helped me realize was that we have the power to choose who and what we allow into our lives. The people we interact with can either uplift us or bring us down. And this choice isn't just important, it's essential for our growth and well-being.

Librarian Sir radiated a type of energy that lifted those around him. Spending time with him, I learned that positivity isn't just an abstract idea, it's real, tangible, and contagious. The company we keep plays a pivotal role in how we perceive the world and how we react to challenges. I soon realized that positivity is something you can absorb, reflect, and share. It spreads through you and encourages others to embrace it too.

We often underestimate how deeply the people in our lives affect us. Have you ever noticed how being around someone positive can instantly lift your spirits, while spending time with someone negative can leave you feeling drained? Energy is contagious, and who we choose to surround ourselves with matters. Positive influences are those who encourage us to grow, celebrate our successes, and provide constructive feedback. They challenge us to be the best version of ourselves.

On the flip side, negative influences can have the opposite effect. Toxic relationships, pessimistic colleagues, and individuals who drain our energy can reinforce limiting beliefs and hold us back. While distancing yourself from negative people can be difficult, especially when they are close friends or family, recognizing their impact is the first step toward reclaiming your mental energy and well-being.

It's not just people that can be positive influences. Books, podcasts, mentors, and even social media accounts that promote growth and positivity can have a profound impact. The key is to intentionally expose yourself to content and interactions that align with your goals and values. The more you surround yourself with positivity, the more it shapes your mindset.

But creating a circle of positive influences isn't just about benefiting from others; it's about becoming that positive influence yourself. By embodying the positivity, kindness, and gratitude that you receive from others, you create a ripple effect. You can inspire and lift others by the example you set. It's not about preaching, it's about living your truth in a way that motivates others to do the same.

Surrounding yourself with positive influences is a proactive choice. It doesn't happen by accident. You have to be intentional about the people you invite into your life and the environments you engage with. This might mean seeking mentors who inspire you, spending more time with friends who motivate you, or consuming content that helps you grow. It might also mean setting boundaries with people or situations that drain you, even if that feels uncomfortable in the short term.

Just as important as the energy you absorb from others is the energy you bring to the table. How are you influencing those around you? Are you adding to the positivity, or contributing to the negativity? By being mindful of the energy you radiate, you can contribute to creating a more positive environment for yourself and others.

Choosing positive influences doesn't mean you only surround yourself with people who are happy all the time. It means finding individuals who are constructive, emotionally supportive, and invested in your growth. These are the relationships that will push you toward becoming the best version of yourself.

Steve Jobs and the Apple Team: Steve Jobs was known for his unique leadership style, one that encouraged creativity, innovation, and challenging the status quo. He intentionally surrounded himself with individuals who were not only highly skilled but who could push him to think outside the box. By creating a team of individuals who inspired and challenged him, Jobs was able to lead Apple to become one of the most successful and innovative companies in history.

Michelle Obama's Supportive Circle: Michelle Obama has often spoken about the importance of surrounding herself with positive, supportive people throughout her life. She credits her strong friendships and close-knit family for helping her navigate the challenges of being First Lady. In her memoir *Becoming*, she talks about the role her mother, friends, and mentors played in her success, emphasizing how vital it is to surround yourself with individuals who uplift you.

Practical Steps:

- **Evaluate relationships**: Spend time with people who lift you up and inspire you to grow.
- **Seek mentors**: Identify individuals who motivate and challenge you to be better.
- **Limit negativity**: Set boundaries with people or situations that drain your energy.

Key Takeaways

The people we surround ourselves with have a profound impact on our lives. By intentionally seeking out positive influences, whether through relationships, mentors, or content, we can shape our mindset and experiences for the better. It's equally important to recognize the energy we bring into spaces, striving to be a source of light for others. Surround yourself with those who challenge, support, and inspire you, and be that positive force in the lives of others.

Lesson 14

The Power of Positive Thinking – A Deeper Exploration

"True power lies not in ignoring hardship, but in choosing hope, positive thinking lights the path through life's darkest moments."

The lesson of positive thinking from Librarian Sir goes beyond merely "thinking happy thoughts." It's about understanding the deep truth that our minds hold immense power over the way we experience life. Positive thinking isn't about denying challenges or pretending everything is perfect; it's about shifting our perspective and focusing on what we can control, our thoughts.

How Our Thoughts Shape Our Reality

Everything in our lives, both good and bad, begins as a thought. Our thoughts lead to feelings, and our feelings drive our actions. Whether we realize it or not, the thoughts we think repeatedly chart the course for our lives. If we constantly think we're unlucky or doomed to fail, we begin to attract more of those outcomes simply because we believe them to be true.

Conversely, when we choose to think positively, focusing on solutions, opportunities, and gratitude, we start to shift our internal world. This shift eventually shows up in our external reality. Our mindset becomes the lens through which we experience life.

The Role of Focus

Librarian Sir taught me a powerful lesson: *"Your focus determines your reality."* In a world filled with negativity, challenges, and hardships, focusing on the good, no matter how small, can transform everything. This isn't about ignoring reality, but choosing to see it through a more constructive lens.

Think of your mind as a spotlight. Whatever you focus on gets amplified. If you focus on the good, you attract more good. If you focus on the bad, the negative energy only grows. By deliberately choosing to focus on the positives, no matter how small, you rewire your brain. You shift from scarcity and despair to abundance and hope.

The Transformative Power of Gratitude

One of the most impactful practices Librarian Sir encouraged me to adopt was gratitude. Focusing on what we are thankful for, no matter how minor, can dramatically shift our mindset. This is where the true power of positive thinking lies, not in ignoring difficulties, but in finding moments of gratitude amidst them.

For example, when you face a tough situation, instead of dwelling on what's going wrong, take a moment to recognize what's still going right. It could be something as simple as a supportive friend, a warm cup of coffee, or the fact that you're still here. Over time, this simple act of looking for the good changes your perspective. You begin to see more reasons to be grateful. You shift from a mindset of lack to one of abundance.

The Ripple Effect of Positive Thinking

The benefits of positive thinking extend beyond just yourself. When you shift your mindset, you create a ripple effect. Your positive energy affects those around you, inspiring them to think more optimistically. It's a domino effect, positivity spreads.

This becomes especially important when surrounded by negative influences. It's easy to get pulled into others' negativity, but maintaining your positive outlook sets an example. The people around you may begin to adopt a more positive mindset themselves, creating a more harmonious and supportive environment.

The Reality of Change: Small Shifts Lead to Big Results

Librarian Sir didn't promise instant change or overnight transformations. Instead, he offered a simple yet powerful shift: focus on the positive. The beauty of this approach lies in its simplicity. It doesn't require drastic changes; it only takes intentionality in where you place your attention.

Over time, these small shifts add up and lead to profound transformations. As you continually reinforce the habit of focusing on the positive, you start to rewire your brain. The more you focus on the good, the more it becomes a natural part of your mindset. Eventually, this shift becomes permanent, and you begin approaching challenges with a mindset of possibility, not defeat.

Jim Carrey's Visualization: Comedian and actor Jim Carrey is a prime example of using the power of positive thinking and visualization. Carrey famously wrote himself a check for $10 million for "acting services rendered," dated Thanksgiving 1995. He kept it in his wallet and visualized receiving that amount. In 1994, Carrey received a $10 million paycheck for his role in *Dumb and Dumber*. His story is a testament to the power of belief, focus, and visualizing success.

Practical Steps:

1. Practice Gratitude: Each morning, list three things you're grateful for.

Starting your day with gratitude can dramatically shift your mindset. By focusing on the positive aspects of your life, no matter how small, you set a tone of abundance and appreciation. Each morning, take a few moments to reflect on three things you're grateful for. This simple practice helps you cultivate a habit of positive thinking, reinforcing the idea that there is always something good in your life, even in challenging times.

2. Use Affirmations: Look in the mirror and affirm your self-worth.

Affirmations are powerful tools that help reprogram your subconscious mind. By speaking positive statements about yourself, you reinforce your self-worth and capabilities. Every morning, stand in front of the mirror, look yourself in the eyes, and repeat affirmations like "I am worthy," "I am capable," or "I am enough." Over time, this helps to build confidence, reduce self-doubt, and shift your internal narrative towards self-belief.

3. Visualize Success: Picture yourself achieving your goals and overcoming obstacles with ease.

Visualization is a technique used by many successful people to manifest their dreams. By vividly imagining yourself achieving your goals and overcoming challenges, you train your mind to believe it is possible. Spend a few minutes each day closing your eyes and mentally rehearse succeeding in your endeavours. Whether it's acing an interview, finishing a project, or handling adversity gracefully, this practice helps solidify your vision and makes success feel within reach.

Key Takeaways

Positive thinking isn't about ignoring challenges; it's about shifting your mindset and choosing to focus on the good. Our thoughts shape our reality, and by focusing on what we can control, our mindset, we can create a life filled with opportunities, growth, and abundance. Start with small shifts: practice gratitude, use affirmations, and visualize success. Over time, these changes will rewire your brain, creating a ripple effect of positivity that transforms your life.

Chapter Summary

In this chapter, we integrated the powerful practical exercises from Lessons 11 to 14 to help you take control of your thoughts, build a positive mindset, and take consistent action toward your goals. These exercises are designed to guide you through the process of transforming your internal dialogue, making intentional decisions, and fostering a healthy mindset for lasting change.

1. **Identifying Negative Thought Patterns**: Start by observing your thoughts throughout the day. When negative thoughts arise, acknowledge them without judgment. This awareness is the first step in shifting from a limiting mindset to one of growth and possibility.
2. **Challenging and Replacing Negative Thoughts**: Once you've identified negative patterns, challenge them by asking yourself, "Is this thought true?" and "Is this thought helpful?" Replace the negativity with empowering affirmations or constructive thoughts, such as, "I am capable and can succeed."
3. **Creating a Ritual for Positivity**: Set aside a few minutes each day to practice gratitude or affirmations. Focus on the positive aspects of your life, no matter how small. This practice will help you rewire your brain and make positivity a daily habit, even in the face of adversity.
4. **Breaking Goals Down**: Large goals can often feel overwhelming. Break them into smaller, manageable steps. This approach makes your objectives feel

more achievable, and each small win builds momentum toward the larger goal.

5. **Taking Immediate Action**: Don't wait for the "perfect time." Take immediate action, even if it's a small step, like making a phone call or sending an email. The hardest part is often just starting, but every action, no matter how small, moves you closer to your goal.
6. **Celebrating Progress**: Recognize and celebrate every small success along the way. Acknowledging progress, no matter how minor, helps keep you motivated and reinforces the habit of consistent action.
7. **Evaluating Relationships**: Surround yourself with people who uplift and inspire you to grow. Spend time with those who challenge you to be better and limit exposure to those who drain your energy.
8. **Seeking Mentors**: Find individuals who motivate and challenge you. A mentor provides guidance, support, and accountability, pushing you to grow and achieve your goals.
9. **Limiting Negativity**: Set boundaries with people or situations that drain your energy. Limiting negativity in your life helps you stay focused on the positive and maintain your emotional and mental well-being.
10. **Practicing Gratitude**: Start each day by listing three things you're grateful for. This simple exercise sets a positive tone for your day and helps you shift your focus to the good in your life, fostering a mindset of abundance.
11. **Using Affirmations**: Stand in front of a mirror and affirm your self-worth. By repeating positive

statements about yourself, you reinforce your confidence and reduce self-doubt, slowly shifting your internal dialogue to one of self-belief.

12. **Visualizing Success**: Spend a few minutes each day visualizing yourself succeeding and overcoming obstacles. Visualization is a powerful technique that helps you mentally prepare for challenges and reinforces your belief that success is within your reach.

These practical steps will empower you to take full control of your thoughts and actions, shifting your mindset toward positivity, growth, and achievement. By cultivating a daily practice of gratitude, affirmations, and goal-setting, you're laying the groundwork for lasting transformation and success.

As you move forward, you'll continue to embrace these practices while stepping into the next phase of your journey: Embracing the Unknown, Building Emotional Strength, and Taking Courageous Action. In Chapter 4, we'll explore how to walk away from toxic situations, overcome fear, and build the life you've always envisioned. This chapter will help you cultivate the courage to stand alone and create a life grounded in self-belief, emotional strength, and personal empowerment. It's time to take everything you've learned and use it to build the future you deserve.

Section: 4

A Day that Changed Everything

It was September 22, 2018, a day etched forever in my mind. It was one of those mornings when everything felt like it was moving along in a simple, familiar routine. The sky was cloudy, the air was cool, and everything seemed normal. But I did not know, this would be the day that would change my life forever.

Just a month before, I had resigned from my job in the merchant navy college. I had worked there for years, but something inside me yearned for something more; more growth, more stability, and a change that could help me create a future beyond the boundaries of that merchant navy company. So, I made the decision to move into a new role in the accounts department of an automobile company. The pressure was immense, the salary was good, but it was a big leap. One that I hoped would eventually bring me the career I dreamed of.

In the midst of this shift, I also made another decision. One that seemed like a simple, harmless idea at the time, but turned out to be a lifeline. My best friend Miera, who was studying law in Dehradun, had come back home after her semester ended. It had been months since we last met because of my job and her studies. I missed her terribly, and we both needed a way to reconnect.

We decided to start taking morning walks together. It would be simple: we'd walk, chat for 10-15 minutes, and go back to our homes. It seemed like the perfect plan. A moment of peace, a chance to breathe, and the joy of being able to see each other regularly.

The night before that fateful day, I mentioned the plan to my father. He didn't say much, just a quiet "Okay." I didn't expect any more reaction. That morning, after some warm up exercises, I was ready to go. I told my mom I was heading out for a walk. She didn't respond. It wasn't unusual. Her silence, after all, had been a constant in my life.

But that morning was different. Little did I know that this walk would be the beginning of an emotional storm I could never have prepared for.

The weather was cloudy, as if it sensed the tension that lay ahead. I had my shoes on and was about to head out when I felt a sense of calmness wash over me. I was 21, in a new job, with new aspirations. The walk with Miera was meant to be a small, simple break in the chaos of life. But as I left my house, I felt a kind of unease that I couldn't explain.

Miera and I met as planned, in the middle of the path, under the same cloudy sky. We laughed, chatting about our lives, our days, and how long it had been since we last spent time together. But then, without warning, the rain began. First, it was a drizzle, then it quickly became a torrential downpour.

Miera, ever the smart one, had brought an umbrella. She suggested we walk together under it, and I agreed. I didn't want to get soaked, and I knew that if I didn't go back soon, the rain would only get worse. We decided to walk back to my house, where I figured we could take shelter for a bit until the storm passed.

When we arrived, the atmosphere in the house was far from welcoming. My mother, who had been in a particularly bad mood for days, was visibly angry. I didn't understand why she was so upset; after all, it was a typical day, one of those mornings where she would yell at me for the smallest things, where I would quietly bear her harsh words. But this time, it felt different. This time, Miera was with me.

As we walked inside, my mom, without any provocation, began to yell at me. The words that came out of her mouth were nothing short of cruel. "You're useless, a slut, a burden who does nothing but wander the streets. You don't even have the decency to stay home and help your family," she shouted. Every word stung, but I had heard worse. This wasn't new to me.

Miera sat quietly, unsure of what to do, her eyes wide in shock. She had never witnessed this side of my family. To her, it was unimaginable that a mother could treat her daughter this way. But for me, it was my reality;

something I had grown numb to, though I still couldn't shake the pain of it.

Then, in a split second, the situation escalated. My mother stormed into the room, and before I could even react, she slapped me hard across the face. My heart raced. It was as though time stood still. The pain was sharp, but the humiliation was what hurt the most. Not because I had been slapped, but because it was happening in front of Miera - my best friend, someone who had never witnessed such cruelty in her own life.

Miera's face turned pale. She looked from me to my mother, unable to process what was happening. I could see the fear in her eyes, but she remained silent, caught in the confusion of it all. My mother wasn't done. She punched me in the back, screamed more vulgar words, and threatened that when my father came home, I would be punished even more severely. "You'll learn your lesson then, you ungrateful bitch," she spat. I stood there, numb, tears welling up in my eyes, but I refused to let them fall. I couldn't let Miera see me break. Not now.

I turned to her, trying to maintain my composure. "Let's just go. We don't need to stay here." I barely managed to say the words. My hands were shaking, my body still in shock. I went to the kitchen, ignoring the pain in my body, and began to make tea for my friend. As I did, I could feel my anger rising. Why was I letting her do this? Why was I accepting it, yet again?

And then, my mother did something that pushed me over the edge. She came into the kitchen, grabbed the tea from my hands, and threw it into the sink. I could feel the heat of the tea splashing onto my skin, but it was nothing compared to the rage building inside me.

"That's it," I said, my voice trembling but resolute. "Why did you do that? Why are you treating me like this?"

My mother, without a second thought, hurled more vulgar insults at me. That was the breaking point. I couldn't take it anymore. With the anger surging through my veins, I knew that this was it. I couldn't stay in this toxic home any longer.

I packed a bag, grabbed my clothes, a pair of shoes, my educational documents and my favourite book. I didn't know where I was going, but I knew I had to leave. Miera was in shock, standing there, unsure of how to react. She hadn't seen this side of my family, hadn't been exposed to the daily abuse I endured. I could see the fear in her eyes as she watched me pack.

The rain outside was now pouring relentlessly, but that didn't matter. We had to go. I couldn't stay. My mother stood at the door, her voice filled with venom: "Go to hell. Never come back. I don't want to see your face again."

With those words ringing in my ears, I walked out the door. The rain was heavy, the road flooded, but it didn't matter. My anger drowned out everything else. Miera held the umbrella over me, trying to shield me from the downpour, but I didn't care. I let the rain soak me, let it wash over the tears I refused to shed.

The streets were empty, except for a few people here and there. The old woman who ran the shop at the end of the street looked at us with concern. I could tell from her eyes that she knew something was wrong. But I didn't care. I had never felt more free in my life.

We walked to the library, drenched but determined. We sat in the common study area, both of us trying to process the madness of the day. I waited for a call from my father, knowing that he would demand an explanation. But as two hours passed, there was no call. My hope dwindled. But as the clock struck around 11 AM, my phone rang. The name on the screen sent a wave of dread through me. It was my father.

I answered, knowing I had to speak, though my voice trembled with fear and emotion. "Hello," I said softly.

"Where are you?" came his voice, cold and demanding.

"In the library," I managed to say, trying to sound calm, but the tears were already welling up.

And then I said the words that I had been holding back for so long: "Papa, Mamma has beaten me today."

The line went silent. I expected some response, some sign that he cared. But instead, he hung up the phone without a word. No questions. No attempt to understand. No concern for his daughter. He just hung up.

I stood there, the phone in my hand, my heart racing in my chest. It wasn't the first time my father had ignored my pain, but this time felt different. I wanted to scream, to break down and call out to him, but I couldn't. He had made it clear that I didn't matter.

Miera, who was sitting beside me, saw the anguish in my eyes. She was furious at what had just happened. She could see the injustice, the cruelty of the situation. "Simran, come with me," she insisted. "You don't deserve this. Let's go. Come to my place. You'll be safe there."

But I hesitated. I wanted to go. I wanted to escape. But deep down, there was a knot of fear inside me. I had nowhere to go. I had no money, no bank account, nothing. I had no real support. Miera could offer me a place to stay, but I couldn't let her take on my burden. I couldn't risk putting her in the same toxic situation I had been living in.

By 6 PM, I realized that no one from my family was going to reach out. I had been abandoned, just as I feared.

After leaving the library after 6 PM, we headed straight to Miera's home. Her mother greeted us with open arms, her kindness giving me a sense of peace and safety that I hadn't felt in a long time. I could feel the warmth of her welcome as she offered me a meal, her soothing presence helping me calm down. I hadn't realized how desperately I needed comfort until I was surrounded by it. As I sat down for dinner, I could finally breathe again, away from the chaos of my own home. It was the first time in days that I felt relaxed, safe, and cared for.

But my fleeting sense of calm was shattered when my father arrived.

It was around 8:30 PM when the doorbell rang. Miera's mother opened it, and I heard my father's voice in the hallway. He wasn't there to apologize or check on me; he was there to attack, to talk behind my back, to drag me through the mud in front of someone else. I could feel the tension rise as he spoke to Miera's mother, making accusations and casting blame. He was trying to twist the story, to make me look like the villain.

"She hit her mother," he said, "She's out of control. She's a danger to herself and everyone around her."

Miera, who had been silent until now, spoke up. "That's not true. I was there. I saw everything. Simran did not hit anyone. It was her mother who did this to her."

But my father didn't care about the truth. He wasn't there to listen. He went on spouting nonsense about fate, astrology, and his so-called "solutions" to everything. When Miera's mother refused to agree with him, my father's true colours came out. He said something that cut deeper than anything else he had said.

"If you leave, that's fine. Whether you stay here or go anywhere in the world, it's your choice," he said coldly. "I won't tell you to come back. I won't beg you."

I stood there, feeling numb, hearing those words that I had long been afraid of. At that moment, I realized that there was no way back. No way to fix the relationship I had with my family. He had just given me the freedom I had been searching for, even if it was wrapped in pain.

But then my father turned to Miera's mother, and the words that followed made my stomach churn. "If you had to choose between your daughter and your husband, who would you choose?" he asked.

Miera's mother answered, "It's not even a question. Both are equally dear to me, and I could never betray either."

To that, my father coldly replied, "Well, in my case, I will always choose my wife, no matter who is right or wrong."

I stood there, frozen. I couldn't believe what I was hearing. My father was telling me, in no uncertain terms, that he would always side with my mother, no matter what. No matter the truth. No matter what had happened.

When my father left, he turned to Miera and said, "When her drama ends, tell her to come back home." But he never said those words to me. He spoke to her, as if I wasn't even there.

Miera, after the door closed behind him, looked at me, her face full of concern. "Simran," she said softly, "this is what your dad said."

That's when it hit me. I had no place to go. No one to turn to. I had been abandoned, not just by my mother, but by my father too. There was no turning back now.

Four days passed without a word from anyone in my family. My father didn't call. My mother didn't reach out. My younger sisters couldn't even contact me, as they didn't have phones. The silence was deafening. And I knew, deep down, that I was on my own now.

Miera, who had always been there for me, didn't hesitate to offer me a way out. She suggested I join her in Dehradun, where she was studying for her law exams. "Come with me," she said. "You'll find a job there. You can start fresh. And if you want, you can send money to your family every month."

I thought about it. A new life, a new city, a fresh start. It seemed like the only way out. Everything was fine. Miera and I did shopping for me and we decided that I will move with her to Dehradun. Just a day before our departure, I received a fateful call from my father.

"When are you coming back?" he demanded.

"I'm not coming back," I replied, my voice firm for the first time in ages.

"You have 30 minutes," he warned. "Come back now, or I'll have you married off next week. You won't have a choice."

I refused both the choices and made my decision clear. I said this while crying "I am not coming and not getting married either."

After listening to me, He gave me an ultimatum, "if you don't want to come back then go to the court and sign an affidavit severing all ties with the family, or return home and accept my decision."

He taunted me. He knew I was too weak to stand up for myself, but that taunt only fueled something deep within me. I would not go back. I would not let him control me any longer. I would survive.

I didn't hesitate. I chose the court. I couldn't go back. I couldn't let them control my life anymore. Just after receiving that call, in 20 minutes, we were in the court.

Miera was the one who helped me navigate the court procedures. I didn't know anything about the legal system, but she took care of everything. She spoke to the lawyers, filled out the forms, and made sure the affidavit was properly attested. She did everything for me. All these court procedures happened within 2 hours of receiving the call from my father. And as we sat in the waiting area of the court, I held the affidavit in my hands; proof that I had taken the first step toward freedom.

Miera turned to me and said, "Simran, stay here. I'll be right back. I need to speak with the lawyer about what we should do next."

I sat there, my hands shaking. I looked down at the copy of the affidavit and the 250 rupees that Miera had given me four days ago. I had no one else in this world except for her, and I knew I couldn't let her be dragged into my mess. I couldn't let my parents hurt her too.

I looked up and saw the exit. I knew what I had to do. I had to leave. I couldn't let Miera suffer because of me. I couldn't let her be dragged into the toxic world I had been living in.

With the affidavit in hand, I made my decision. I would leave. I wouldn't tell her. I couldn't.

I ran. I ran through the streets, feeling the cold pavement beneath my torn shoes. I had no money, no support. I had no plan, no future, but I had one thing: the will to survive.

I ran to the nearest bus stop. I bought a ticket to the nearest city, using the last of the money Miera had given me. And as the bus pulled away, I looked out the window, leaving the city behind, leaving my family, leaving everything.

This was the beginning of a new life. A life I had to fight for. A life I had to claim for myself.

My journey wasn't just about escaping the toxicity I had lived with, but about rediscovering myself in a world that had once seemed so hostile and unpredictable. From the moment I walked away, I had no clue what lay ahead. The fear of an unknown future loomed, but in that uncertainty, I found my greatest lesson: sometimes, it takes the chaos of your life falling apart for you to finally see that you have the strength to rebuild it from scratch. In every setback, I found a stepping stone; in every struggle, a chance to redefine myself. It wasn't easy, and there were moments when I wanted to quit, but I learned to embrace the fear and uncertainty, because it was the only way I could start living on my own terms. This is where the power of self-determination came in, pushing me to keep moving forward even when I had nothing but a glimmer of hope. And as I kept walking, it became clear; it wasn't the world around me that needed to change. It was me. And that realization is what connects my story to the lessons that follow. In this journey, I discovered the true essence of strength; not just physical, but emotional. Now, it's time for you to understand that the power to rise above the obstacles in your life isn't something that comes from others; it comes from within. You have the ability to reshape your own reality, just as I did.

Lesson 15

Embracing the Unknown

"Growth begins where certainty ends. Embrace the unknown, and discover your true potential."

In life, we all face moments where we're pushed to the edge of our comfort zones. These are the moments where we must make decisions without knowing the full outcome, where we step into new territories with no guarantees, and leave behind what we once thought was safe and secure. The question becomes: *Will you embrace the unknown, or let fear hold you back?*

The Comfort of the Known

Before I made the decision to leave my family and everything I had known, I was trapped in a cycle of fear. My home was filled with anger and hurt, but it was still *home*. I stayed because it was familiar, despite the emotional pain it caused me.

Leaving, however, was the most uncertain thing I could do. I had no backup plan, just a small sum of money, a legal affidavit, and a torn pair of shoes. In that moment, I had to embrace the unknown. I had no map, no promises, only the knowledge that I couldn't stay in the life I was living.

The Fear of the Unknown

The hardest part of embracing the unknown is the fear that accompanies it. The weight of uncertainty can be suffocating. When I left, I had no idea where I was going or how I would survive. But it was in that fear that I made the choice to *trust myself*. Fear is natural, but it doesn't have to control your decisions. Embracing the unknown doesn't mean being fearless, it means choosing to trust yourself despite fear.

Trusting the Journey

As I left behind the familiar, I realized something essential: The journey itself is the reward. I didn't need to know the destination. What mattered was that I moved. Even if the path was unclear, taking action was the key. And often, it's not about having everything figured out, it's about having the courage to take that first step, knowing that each step will lead you somewhere new and worthwhile.

The Growth That Comes from Uncertainty

As I moved further from my past, I discovered that the more uncertain my future seemed, the more I was growing. The unknown isn't something to be afraid of; it's a space for reinvention and freedom. When you embrace uncertainty, you open yourself to the possibility of change, of shedding your past and rebuilding yourself, stronger and wiser.

Research on the Benefits of Embracing Uncertainty

Psychologist Tali Sharot in her book *The Optimism Bias* argues that the brain is wired to make us fear uncertainty. However, embracing the unknown is essential for growth. Studies have shown that embracing uncertainty increases creativity, problem-solving abilities, and resilience. People who are comfortable with uncertainty tend to take more risks, which in turn leads to greater opportunities and personal growth. This underscores the importance of developing a mindset that is open to uncertainty as a source of empowerment rather than fear.

Your Moment to Embrace the Unknown

If you find yourself at a crossroads, uncertain of what lies ahead, I want you to know: *You have the power to step into the unknown*. You don't need to have it all figured out. You don't need a plan. You simply need to take that first step, however small it may seem. Trust that the unknown will lead you to places you've never imagined, and that you are capable of handling whatever comes your way.

Practical Steps:

1. **Say "yes" more often:** Push yourself to accept invitations and opportunities that take you out of your comfort zone, even if they seem daunting.
2. **Let go of the need for certainty:** Remind yourself that it's not about having all the answers, it's about taking the next step, even if it's unclear.

3. **Trust the process:** When fear creeps in, repeat: *"I trust the timing of my life."* Let go of the need to control everything, and trust that the journey is unfolding as it should.

The future is waiting for you to create it. Step forward, and embrace the unknown. It's in that space that you will discover your true strength, and unlock opportunities you never thought possible.

Lesson 16

The Strength to Walk Away from Toxicity

"True strength is knowing when to stay and when to leave, walking away from toxicity is reclaiming your peace."

You Deserve Peace

Walking away from toxicity isn't just a decision; it's an act of courage, a declaration of self-worth. Whether it's a toxic relationship, environment, or internal belief, releasing what drains you is the first step toward reclaiming your power.

I remember the moment I left my toxic home. It was messy, heartbreaking, and confusing. But it was also the moment I decided my peace was more valuable than my past.

Toxicity Is a Slow Poison

It often starts quietly. Subtle put-downs, disguised control, love wrapped in guilt. I lived in a house where emotional manipulation was masked as concern, where being beaten down verbally and physically became the norm.

Over time, you begin to believe that this is just life. But here's the truth: **toxic environments are not normal**, and they're not your fault.

The Breaking Point

Sometimes, one moment shatters the illusion. For me, it was after a violent altercation and years of silence from my father. That moment forced me to ask: *Do I want to survive, or do I want to live?*

And that's when I chose myself.

The Fear Is Real, but So Is Your Strength

Letting go is terrifying. You're not just leaving people, you're leaving the version of yourself that tolerated pain. But fear is a compass. It points you toward what needs healing.

According to psychologist Dr. Susan Forward, "Staying in a toxic relationship out of guilt or fear is one of the most damaging things you can do to your mental health" (*Forward, 1997*).

Redefining Loyalty

We're taught to equate love with sacrifice. But enduring pain is not loyalty, its self-abandonment. Choosing yourself doesn't make you selfish. It makes you *whole.*

Guilt will whisper that you're betraying them. But what if staying is betraying yourself?

The Power of Walking Away

When I left, I lost people, but I found myself. The silence that followed was loud, but it was also peaceful. For the first time, I could breathe without fear.

People who walk away from toxic environments report measurable improvements in sleep quality, reduced anxiety, and increased self-worth within months of distancing themselves.

Practical Steps

- **Identify the Source**: Who or what drains your energy? Write it down.
- **Create Space**: Limit or cut off contact. Mute, unfollow, or block if needed.
- **Replace with Growth**: Fill that space, new hobbies, safe friendships, self-care.
- **Affirm Your Choice**: Every day, repeat: *"I am allowed to choose peace."*

Choose peace. Choose power. Choose you.

"You don't get to choose how you're broken, but you do get to choose how you heal."
, Dr. Edith Eger, Holocaust survivor and psychologist

Lesson 17

The Courage to Stand Alone

"The man who goes alone can start today; but he who travels with another must wait till that other is ready." – Henry David Thoreau

Standing alone isn't just about solitude, it's about sovereignty. It's the ability to stand tall in your truth when everything and everyone is pushing you to conform. It's what builds unshakable confidence and clarity. I didn't learn this lesson from a book or a course,I learned it in the silence that followed walking away from everything familiar.

When You Have No One But Yourself

The day I chose to walk away from my toxic family, I wasn't just walking away from people, I was letting go of an entire identity. The silence afterward was deafening. I wasn't used to hearing my own thoughts without the background noise of criticism or control.

But something beautiful happened in that stillness: I started to hear *me*. My voice. My instincts. My dreams.

Viola Davis, now an Oscar-winning actress, grew up in poverty and violence. In her memoir *Finding Me* (2022), she shares how stepping away from her past, including toxic family dynamics and internalized shame, allowed her to define her own future. "I had to stop waiting for someone to come rescue me," she writes. "It was my own rescue plan."

The Fear of Being Misunderstood

When you make a bold move, people will talk. I remember the looks, the whispers, the judgment from others after I left. "You're abandoning your family," they said. "You'll regret this."

But here's the truth: *they weren't living my life*. They didn't feel the pain I did behind closed doors. Choosing to stand alone isn't about rebellion, it's about survival. About choosing peace over performance.

The Strength Within Silence

Silence used to scare me. Now, I crave it. Because when you're standing alone, without the noise of everyone else's opinions, you finally get to figure out what *you* believe. That's not weakness, that's wisdom.

Practical Steps :

- **Set firm boundaries.** Say no once. If it's not respected, you have your answer.
- **Practice solitude.** Take a solo walk, journal, or enjoy a meal alone. Learn to love your own company.
- **Stand unapologetically.** Your peace is not up for debate. You owe no one an explanation for choosing yourself.

Encouragement for You

If you're facing a choice that means standing alone, trust yourself. It's okay to be misunderstood. It's okay to feel lonely. That's where your real strength is born.

The most powerful people you admire, whether it's Oprah, Steve Jobs, or Malala, have all had to walk alone at some point. Not because they wanted to, but because standing alone was the price of standing in their truth.

So here's your reminder: You are not alone in standing alone.

"You'll never find your voice while you're trying to keep everyone else comfortable."

Lesson 18

Overcoming the Fear of the Future

"Fear of the future fades when you anchor yourself in the present"

The future is full of potential, yet heavy with uncertainty. For many, it's not an opportunity we see when we look ahead, but a risk. What if I fail? What if I lose everything? These fears, left unchecked, can stop us from taking the very steps that could transform our lives.

I know the feeling. When I left home, I had no blueprint, no safety net, and no clear direction. Every step felt like walking blindfolded across a tightrope. But standing still out of fear wasn't an option; it was either move or remains stuck forever.

Shift Your Perspective

Instead of seeing the future as a void, try viewing it as a canvas. You don't need the full picture , you only need the courage to paint the first stroke.

Start asking:

- *What can I control right now?*
- *What does moving forward, even imperfectly, look like today?*

Cognitive science backs this: Psychologist Dr. Susan Jeffers famously wrote in her bestselling book *Feel the Fear and Do It Anyway* that "Pushing through fear is less frightening than living with the underlying fear that comes from a feeling of helplessness."

Trust Your Inner Compass

One of the biggest lies fear tells us is: "You're not ready." But readiness isn't a moment, it's a mindset. You don't need certainty to take action. You need self-trust.

When I walked away from everything familiar, I didn't have all the answers. But I trusted my ability to adapt, to learn, and to keep moving forward, and that made all the difference.

Let Go of the Illusion of Control

Trying to control every aspect of the future is like trying to stop the tide with your hands. You can't, and you don't have to. Peace comes when you surrender to the process.

Encouragement for You

If the fear of the future has been whispering "you're not enough," I want you to hear this louder: You are. You don't have to see the entire staircase, just take the next step.

No one has the future figured out. And that's okay. What matters is showing up, even scared. Because the people who move forward are not the ones without fear , they're the ones who act anyway.

Practical Steps:

- **Control the controllable:** Write down what's in your power (e.g., your mindset, actions, effort). Let go of the rest.
- **Flip the fear:** Ask, *What's the worst that could happen?* Then create a "Plan B." Fear shrinks when faced directly.
- **Courage reps:** Do one small, scary thing daily, pitch an idea, apply for the role, and take the leap. Each rep builds resilience.

Lesson 19
The Importance of Self-Belief

"Self-belief is the foundation on which dreams are built and without it, even the brightest visions can falter."

When you're standing at life's crossroads, overwhelmed by uncertainty, there's one power you can always rely on: self-belief. It's the force that steadies you when the world shakes, the inner trust that says, *"I can get through this."*

I've seen firsthand how crucial this is. When I left home, I had no plan, no support system, and just a few rupees to my name. But I had one thing that refused to quit on me, my belief that I could make it, somehow. That belief was my anchor through the chaos.

Why Self-Belief Matters

Self-belief isn't about arrogance or blind optimism. It's about trusting yourself, your decisions, your abilities, your value. It's knowing that even when nothing is guaranteed, you can rely on your own resilience.

When fear crept in, when I thought maybe I had made the biggest mistake of my life, I kept returning to this belief. *If I made it through yesterday, I can survive tomorrow.*

This mindset is not built overnight. It must be reinforced daily. Doubt is natural, but belief must be chosen again and again.

Real-Life Case Study: Howard Schultz

Howard Schultz, the former CEO of Starbucks, grew up in public housing and worked his way up through hardship. When he pitched the idea of Starbucks' espresso bar concept, 217 investors rejected him. But his belief in the vision, and in himself, was unshakable. Eventually, that belief turned Starbucks into a global brand. Schultz once said, "In times of adversity and change, we really discover who we are and what we're made of."

That's the kind of belief that builds something lasting, not just for entrepreneurs, but for anyone trying to change their life.

Self-Belief and Action Go Hand in Hand

Belief alone isn't enough; it has to be backed by action. When I had nothing, I didn't wait for the perfect opportunity. I took messy, uncertain steps forward. Every action was a small vote of confidence in myself.

Self-efficacy, or belief in one's ability to succeed, was a better predictor of performance than actual skill level. In other words: what you believe you can do often matters more than what you *currently* can do.

Obstacles Are Inevitable, But Not Immovable

Life throws curveballs. When my family cut ties with me, when I had no place to sleep, no money to eat, I could've given in. But I didn't. Not because I had answers, but because I believed I could *find* them.

Obstacles stopped being roadblocks and started becoming building blocks.

Self-Belief Is Non-Negotiable

If you want to build a life that's yours, on your terms, self-belief is not optional. People won't always cheer you on. The world won't always reassure you. You must be your own source of courage.

You don't need everyone to believe in you. You just need one person: yourself.

Practical Steps

- **Keep promises to yourself**
  Show yourself you're reliable. If you say you'll do something, do it. Start small and build from there.

- **Visualize your future self**
  Spend 5 minutes each day visualizing success. See it. Feel it. Let it become real in your mind first.

- **Detach from external approval**
  Pause when you find yourself seeking validation. Ask, *"Do I believe in this for me?"* That's what matters.

No matter how uncertain the road, if you believe in yourself, you're already halfway there. Keep moving. Keep believing. Keep becoming.

Lesson 20

Building Your Life from Scratch

"When life strips you down to nothing, it offers a blank canvas, rebuild with colors that are truly yours."

Life has a way of shaking us to our core, and when everything you've known falls apart, it's easy to feel lost. But in these moments, you are handed an incredible gift: the chance to rebuild, reinvent, and create the life you truly desire. Starting over is daunting, but it's also empowering. It is the opportunity to build your life from scratch, free from the weight of past limitations.

In my own life, I've faced that crossroads, standing at the edge with nothing but the pieces of my past scattered before me. No family support, no stability, no clear direction. Yet, in that moment of emptiness, I realized that I had the power to build something new.

The Power of Starting Over

Starting over can feel like standing on the edge of a cliff, unsure if you should leap or step back. But when old life crumbles, you're left with a blank canvas, no rules, no constraints. It's in these moments that your true strength emerges.

The first step to rebuilding is accepting that the future is yours to design. Don't try to rebuild the old life or chase after what's been lost. This is your chance to forge something entirely new. When I decided to walk away from everything, I didn't know how or where to begin. But I knew I couldn't go back. The only way forward was to start from scratch and trust that I could rebuild, piece by piece.

Starting with a Vision

To rebuild, you need a vision. It doesn't have to be grand; just a simple, guiding idea of what your future could look like. For me, it was freedom, freedom from a toxic past and freedom to create my own path. Your vision will guide you through the uncertainty and help you find direction when you're unsure of what comes next.

Don't worry about having everything figured out. The important thing is to take the first step. Trust that the rest will follow.

Steve Jobs' Return to Apple

One of the most famous examples of rebuilding is Steve Jobs' return to Apple. After being ousted from the company he founded, Jobs could have taken it as a failure. Instead, he reinvented himself and Apple. When he returned to the company in 1997, it was on the brink of bankruptcy. Jobs' vision for Apple's future wasn't just about products; it was about creating an ecosystem, fostering creativity, and rethinking the technology industry. He didn't have all the answers when he returned, but he knew that the only way forward was to follow his vision, piece by piece. Under his leadership,

Apple transformed and became one of the most valuable companies in the world.

Finding Strength in the Process

Rebuilding doesn't happen overnight. It's a slow and sometimes painful journey. You'll face moments of doubt, exhaustion, and frustration, but these struggles are part of the process. Each challenge you face and overcome builds your strength and resilience.

On my own journey, when I had only a few rupees in my pocket, I didn't know how I would survive. But I knew that I had no choice but to keep moving forward. Every small victory, no matter how small, was a step closer to my goal. The process of rebuilding is about steady, consistent effort, even on the toughest days.

The Power of Incremental Progress

Research in behavioural science, especially studies around "Kaizen" (Japanese for "continuous improvement"), has shown that small, consistent steps are the most effective way to make big changes in life. A study by Robert Maurer in his book *One Small Step Can Change Your Life* suggests that incremental progress allows you to overcome fear and procrastination, making it easier to tackle larger tasks.

Taking Responsibility for Your Life

Building your life from scratch means taking full responsibility for your future. You have the power to create your own path, but no one will hand it to you. It's up to you to take ownership of your decisions, your actions, and your future.

When I walked away, I had no safety net, no one to tell me what to do. I was forced to rely on myself. And that was empowering. You are the architect of your own future, and the power to shape your life is in your hands.

Building a New Support System

As you rebuild, make sure you surround yourself with people who support your growth. In my journey, I was fortunate to find people who believed in me even when I didn't believe in myself. Find individuals who will challenge you, uplift you, and encourage your progress.

At the same time, be prepared to let go of relationships that hold you back. Rebuilding requires you to let go of what no longer serves you, whether it's toxic relationships, old habits, or limiting beliefs.

Embracing the Process

Rebuilding is not an instant transformation. It takes time, patience, and persistence. There will be moments when it feels like you're making no progress. But each small step you take brings you closer to the life you want. Remember, it's about progress, not perfection. Embrace each step, no matter how small, and trust that you're moving in the right direction.

The Freedom to Create Your Future

The most beautiful part of starting over is the freedom it gives you. You no longer have to live according to others' expectations or the past. You are free to create the life you want. You can reinvent yourself and build a future that aligns with your values and dreams.

When I walked away from everything, I wasn't just leaving the past behind, I was stepping toward a future that was entirely mine to create. And so can you. Your future is waiting for you to take that first step.

Encouragement for You

If you find yourself at a crossroads, unsure of where to begin, remember this: you have the power to create the life you desire. It won't be easy, and it won't happen overnight. But if you have the courage to start, if you keep moving forward, you can create something beautiful and meaningful.

Practical Steps:

- **Clear the wreckage**: Let go of anything or anyone holding you back, old habits, toxic relationships, limiting beliefs.
- **Create a vision board**: Cut out images and words that represent the life you want. Keep it where you'll see it daily.
- **Set micro-goals**: Break down your big vision into small, achievable steps. Celebrate each victory, no matter how small.

- **Expand your circle**: Join groups, clubs, or support networks aligned with your passions and goals. Surround your

- self with people who uplift you.

Lesson 21

Emotional Strength over Physical Strength

"True power isn't in muscle, but in resilience. Emotional strength shapes how we rise after every fall."

In a world that often prizes physical strength and appearance, it can be easy to believe that the strongest among us are those who can lift the heaviest weights or achieve the most visible success. But true strength goes beyond muscle. It lies in the emotional resilience that helps us navigate life's challenges, face pain, and keep moving forward, even when everything seems to be crumbling.

In my journey, there were moments when my physical body was exhausted, and yet it was my emotional resilience that pushed me through. It was the strength to rise after failure, to face rejection, and to keep believing in myself when all I had left was the will to move forward.

The Power of Emotional Resilience

Physical strength has its limits. Our bodies can only take so much before they tire out. But emotional resilience is limitless. It allows us to adapt, recover, and keep going in the face of adversity. It's what helps us endure emotional pain, loss, and fear, coming out stronger on the other side.

Studies show that emotional resilience is key to mental and physical well-being. Emotionally resilient people tend to recover faster from stress and have a better ability to manage their emotions during tough times. Emotional strength is the foundation of true success because it allows us to stay grounded even when everything else around us is chaotic.

Emotional Strength in the Face of Pain

Physical pain can be intense, but emotional pain can be even more excruciating. It's the heartbreak of betrayal, the sting of rejection, or the crushing weight of abandonment. When I left my home, I wasn't just escaping a physical environment, I was leaving behind toxic emotional patterns and relationships that had held me back.

In these moments, it wasn't about physical strength; it was the emotional courage to walk away from what was hurting me. People who develop emotional resilience are more likely to have healthy relationships and recover from setbacks faster. Emotional strength isn't just about surviving; it's about thriving after emotional wounds.

Building Emotional Strength

Emotional strength isn't built in an instant. It grows over time, shaped by the challenges we face and how we choose to respond. Each setback, each heartache, is an opportunity to build resilience.

For me, facing rejection wasn't a reason to give up; it was an opportunity to grow stronger. Every painful moment was like a weight that strengthened my emotional muscle.

Emotional Strength in Decision Making

Some decisions demand emotional strength more than physical strength. Walking away from toxic relationships, for instance, requires clarity, courage, and emotional resilience. It's not about fighting battles head-on, it's about knowing when to step back for your mental and emotional health.

When I made the difficult decision to leave everything behind, it wasn't about physical endurance; it was about the clarity and courage to choose my well-being over fear. This kind of emotional strength isn't about avoiding conflict; it's about protecting your peace and aligning your actions with your values.

Overcoming Self-Doubt

One of the most challenging aspects of building emotional strength is overcoming self-doubt. We all have moments when we question ourselves. When I started over, I often wondered if I was making the right choices. But it was my emotional resilience, the ability to quiet the voice of doubt that helped me keep moving forward.

Encouragement for You

If you're facing a challenge that seems insurmountable, remember that emotional strength will carry you through. It's not about how much weight you can lift or how physically strong you are. It's about how you manage the emotional challenges life throws at you. You have the power within you to endure, to rise above, and to keep moving forward, even when the road is tough.

You are stronger than you realize. Your emotional strength is the key to creating the life you want, and with each passing day, you'll build even more resilience. Embrace the small victories, and know that they will lead you to your ultimate goals.

Practical Steps:

- **Practice emotional regulation**: When overwhelmed, pause. Take 5 deep breaths: inhale through your nose for 4 counts, hold for 4, and exhale for 4.
- **Reframe challenges**: See struggles as opportunities for growth. Ask yourself: "What is this teaching me?"
- **Celebrate emotional wins**: Each time you handle a situation with calm and self-control, celebrate it. Recognizing small victories builds emotional resilience.

Chapter Summary

In this final chapter, we've woven together the key practical exercises from Lessons 15 to 21, providing you with a comprehensive toolkit to build emotional strength, overcome self-doubt, and embrace the unknown. These lessons have been designed to empower you to take courageous action, face your fears head-on, and transform your emotional resilience into lasting change.

1. **Recognizing and Facing Fear**: Start by identifying the fears that are holding you back. Acknowledge them without judgment and take gradual steps to face them. With each small challenge, you reduce the power fear has over you, gaining confidence along the way.

2. **Emotional Regulation**: Practice emotional regulation by taking a pause when faced with stress. Deep breathing and awareness of your emotional state will help you stay grounded and composed, allowing you to respond rather than react in difficult situations.

3. **Reframing Negative Thoughts**: Challenge your negative thoughts by asking yourself, "What is this teaching me?" Shift your mindset to see challenges as opportunities for growth, reinforcing the belief that you can rise above any adversity.

4. **Celebrating Small Emotional Wins**: Recognize and celebrate moments where you handle emotionally difficult situations with resilience. These small

victories compound over time, building emotional strength and reinforcing the habit of responding with grace.

5. **Gratitude Practice**: Begin each day by listing three things you're grateful for. This simple practice shifts your focus from fear and negativity to abundance and positivity, fostering a mindset of strength and growth.

6. **Making Empowered Decisions**: Trust your emotional clarity when making tough decisions. Sometimes this means walking away from toxic situations or relationships that no longer serve you. Emotional strength lies in knowing when to choose your well-being over the comfort of familiarity.

7. **Combating Self-Doubt**: Recognize that self-doubt is a natural part of growth. Take action despite the doubt, knowing that each step you take strengthens your emotional resilience and your belief in your capabilities.

8. **Visualization**: Dedicate a few minutes each day to visualize yourself overcoming obstacles and achieving your goals. This practice not only prepares you mentally for challenges but also reinforces the emotional strength you need to tackle them.

9. **Setting Boundaries**: Protect your emotional health by setting clear and firm boundaries. Limit your exposure to negativity and prioritize relationships that nurture and support your growth.

10. **Using Affirmations**: Affirm your self-worth daily. Positive affirmations will gradually reprogram your mind, reducing self-doubt and reinforcing your belief in your ability to handle life's challenges with resilience.

By embracing these exercises, you're equipped to rise above the challenges that life presents. Emotional strength is your foundation, and with each passing day, it becomes stronger and more ingrained within you.

As you continue your journey beyond this book, remember that emotional resilience isn't a one-time achievement; it's a continuous practice that will guide you through the inevitable ups and downs of life. With courage, clarity, and emotional strength, you have the power to create the life you've always desired, one where your inner strength defines your reality, not external circumstances.

Now it's time to take action. The life you deserve is waiting for you.

Final Ending

As you turn the final page of this book, know that the journey you've just completed is only the beginning. You've stepped into your own power, faced your fears, and discovered a deeper strength within yourself. The lessons you've absorbed, the insights you've gained, and the tools you've learned are the building blocks for the life you deserve. But more importantly, you've awakened to the truth that the real strength lies not in what we can see or touch, but in what we feel, believe, and choose to carry forward.

True transformation is not about perfection, but about progress. It's about the courage to rise every time you fall, the resilience to keep moving forward despite the obstacles, and the commitment to remain true to yourself in every moment.

You now know that emotional strength, self-belief, and perseverance are the pillars that will carry you through any storm. You are not defined by your circumstances, nor by the challenges you've faced. You are defined by the power you have to choose, to change, and to create the life you want.

As you move forward, remember that the path you've begun is one that requires consistent effort, but also immense grace. It's okay to stumble, to have moments of doubt, or to feel uncertain about the road ahead. What matters most is your unwavering commitment to keep going, to rise above the noise, and to trust in your own abilities.

Your journey of self-discovery and growth doesn't end here. In fact, it's only just beginning. Every new step you take will unlock more of your potential, more of your strength, and more of the extraordinary life you were meant to live. The power to create the life you envision is already within you, waiting for you to claim it.

So, take a deep breath and step forward with confidence. You've already begun the process of transformation. Now, continue it with courage, belief, and the knowledge that your emotional strength is the foundation for everything that is to come.

You are enough. You are worthy. And you are unstoppable.

The world is waiting for you to show up, to be your true self, and to live a life that aligns with your deepest desires.

The journey to the life you've always dreamed of begins now.

Note to My Readers

Thank you so much for taking the time to read "Because I Never Give Up." I hope the lessons shared within these pages have inspired you to tap into your own resilience and emotional intelligence. If this book has made a difference for you**, I would be incredibly grateful if you could leave a review on Amazon.** Your feedback not only helps me grow as a writer, but it also helps others discover this book and begin their own journey of personal growth.

Follow me on Instagram.

Stay connected and keeps the conversation going! I'd love to hear your thoughts, insights, and how you're applying the principles of emotional intelligence and resilience in your life. Follow me at ***@authorsimrank.saini*** for updates, motivational tips, and more!

Thank you again for your support, and remember , you never have to give up on becoming the best version of yourself.

References

Achor, S. (2010). The Happiness Advantage. Crown Publishing.
American Psychological Association. (2019). Emotional Resilience Resource. APA.
Angelou, M. (1969). I Know Why the Caged Bird Sings. Random House.
Bandura, A. (1977). Self-Efficacy: Toward a Unifying Theory of Behavioral Change. Psychological Review.
Bonanno, G. A. (2017). Resilience in the Face of Trauma. Psychological Science.
Brown, B. (2010). The Gifts of Imperfection. Hazelden Publishing.
Brown, B. (2012). Daring Greatly. Gotham Books.
Clear, J. (2018). Atomic Habits. Avery.
Davis, V. (2022). Finding Me. HarperOne.
Dweck, C. (2006). Mindset: The New Psychology of Success. Random House.
Eger, E. (2017). The Choice. Scribner.
Emmons, R. A., & McCullough, M. E. (2003). Counting Blessings Versus Burdens. Journal of Personality and Social Psychology.
Enright, R. D. (2001). Forgiveness is a Choice: A Step-by-Step Process for Resolving Anger and Restoring Hope. American Psychological Association.
Finkel, E. J., & Eastwick, P. W. (2015). Interpersonal Attraction. APA Handbook.
Forward, S. (1997). Emotional Blackmail. HarperCollins.
Fredrickson, B. L. (2009). Positivity. Crown Publishing Group.
Gilbert, E. (2015). Big Magic. Riverhead Books.
Goleman, D. (1995). Emotional Intelligence: Why It Can Matter More Than IQ. Bantam Books.
Harvard Health Publishing. (n.d.). Fostering Healthy Relationships. Harvard Health.
Haskell, R. (2018). Serena Williams on Motherhood, Marriage, and Making Her Comeback. Vogue.
Isaacson, W. (2011). Steve Jobs. Simon & Schuster.
Jeffers, S. (1987). Feel the Fear and Do It Anyway. Ballantine Books.
Kabat-Zinn, J. (1990). Full Catastrophe Living. Delta Publishing.
Leary, M. R. (2007). Self-Esteem. Current Directions in Psychological Science.
Luskin, F. (2002). Forgive for Good. HarperOne.
Lyubomirsky, S. (2008). The How of Happiness. Penguin Press.
Masten, A. S. (2001). Resilience in Children. Journal of Developmental and Behavioral Pediatrics.
Masten, A. S. (2018). Resilience in Children and Adolescents. Journal of Positive Psychology.
Maurer, R. (2004). One Small Step Can Change Your Life. Workman Publishing.
Neff, K. (2011). Self-Compassion: The Proven Power of Being Kind to Yourself. William Morrow.
Obama, M. (2018). Becoming. Crown Publishing Group.
Pennebaker, J. W. (1997). Writing About Emotional Experiences as a Therapeutic Process. Psychological Science.
Rowling, J. K. (2008). The Fringe Benefits of Failure. Harvard Commencement Speech.
Schultz, H. (2011). Onward. Rodale Books.
Seligman, M. E. P. (2011). Flourish. Free Press.
Sharot, T. (2011). The Optimism Bias. Pantheon Books.
Smithsonian Institution. (n.d.). Edison Light Bulb. Smithsonian.
Tedeschi, R. G., & Calhoun, L. G. (2004). Post-Traumatic Growth. Psychology Press.
Thunberg, G. (2019). No One Is Too Small to Make a Difference. Penguin.
Tolle, E. (1999). The Power of Now. New World Library.
Toussaint, L., & Williams, D. R. (2008). Forgiveness and Health. Journal of Social and Clinical Psychology.
Winfrey, O. (2014). Oprah's Lifeclass. Oprah Winfrey Network.
Worthington, E. L. (2001). Forgiveness and Reconciliation. Springer Publishing.
Yousafzai, M. (2013). I Am Malala. Little, Brown and Company.

www.ingramcontent.com/pod-product-compliance
Lightning Source LLC
Chambersburg PA
CBHW062139160726
48282CB00027B/878
9789334288735